Authentic Kindness

Praise for
AUTHENTIC KINDNESS

"The root of the word kindness is "kin" or relation. In an era of retribalization, Barbara Gulbranson is calling us to a fresh realization of our connectedness that is not only key to individual health and vitality, but to the survival of the human race. In this gem of a book, Barbara not only inspires us to engage "authentic kindness" through the stories of transformed and transforming individuals, she gives us practical steps for living into that heart expanding reality. Her writing is itself an expression of authentic kindness to the rest of us who are hungry for hope and connection."

FE ANAM AVIS, Creator of Soul Shop™
Ministering to those Impacted by Suicidal Desperation

"If the current culture of insult and attack troubles you, this book will restore your faith in humanity. In my 40 years working with spiritual seekers, this is the first book I've found that makes authentic kindness understandable and accessible. The book shares a clear understanding of the nature of kindness, along with practical tips and affirmations to cultivate its presence in everyday life."

REV. DON CHATFIELD, Ph.D., Executive Director
Osage Forest of Peace

"For my friend, Barbara, I think this book was clearly a labor of love. I have no doubt that for the reader it will be an awakening of the Spirit. It affirms the goodness of which humanity is capable and shows us the "how to" of living by integrating kindness and compassion into our very being. It is these two attributes that can heal the world. Through her work Barbara has shown us this better way to think, to feel, and to conduct ourselves daily. By practicing these we will be happier, better individuals, capable of being true friends to all sentient beings and helping to alleviate suffering wherever we find it."

KIRBY L. WHITACRE, author of
Buddhism, A Westerner's Compendium

"This book exemplifies the magnificent universal principles that ensure the manifestation of a joy-filled, health-driven abundant life. A must read!"

DR ANGELO PIZELO
President of the Emerson Theological Institute and
Spiritual Leader of the Emerson New Thought Center

"*Authentic Kindness* is a real gem. With thoughtful insight Barbara Gulbranson takes you by the hand and gently leads you through the healing and restorative power of kindness. Beautifully written, the stories along with the suggested practices offer a profound experience in shifting your awareness of the power of kindness to heal one's self with the side effect of enriching another's life. As a spiritual coach, I will recommend this book to all my clients. A brilliant piece of work!"

DR JANINE H. BURNS, Director of the Guiding Light
Foundation creator of *Tunes for Transformation*

"There is only one purpose in life – to help others. *Authentic Kindness: The Path to Peace, Love and Joy* offers many great ways to live a purposeful life."

C. NORMAN SHEALY, M.D., Ph. D.
Founder and CEO, International Institute of Holistic Medicine
Co-Founder, American Board of Scientific Medical Intuition
Editor *Journal of Comprehensive Integrative Medicine*
Tiwehkt, Native American Church of Nemenhah
President, Holos Energy Medicine Eudcation
Professor Emeritus, of Energy Medicine, Holos University
Graduate Seminary

"The message in *Authentic Kindness: The Path to Peace, Love, and Joy* by Barbara Gulbranson could not have been shared at a better time. We as humans are sharing many different experiences daily and this book is an inspiration and a guide for many. I have been honored to share Barbara's messages via my radio show and am looking forward to featuring her words of wisdom from this meaningful book to my listeners. Congratulations, Barbara, and keep up the good work."

CAROLE MATTHEWS, Intuitive Medium
Radio host of the Carole Matthews Show

Authentic Kindness

The Path to Peace, Love and Joy

BARBARA GULBRANSON

Monarch Press
Granger, Indiana

Copyright 2017 © by Barbara Gulbranson

All rights reserved. No part of this book may be reproduced or transmitted in any form by any means, electronic or mechanical, including photocopying, recording, or by any information storage and retrieval system, without permission in writing of the publisher.

Care has been taken to trace the ownership and obtain permission, if necessary, for excerpts from the works of others. If any errors have occurred, they will be corrected in subsequent printings provided notification is sent to the publisher.

The author has changed the names and identifying characteristics of all persons whose experiences are included in the book to protect their privacy, except for those who consented to using their real names. Any similarity between fictitious names used and those of living persons is entirely coincidental.

Library of Congress Control Number:
ISBN: 978-1-970024-67-8

Printed in the United States of America

Published by
Monarch Press
P.O. Box 1045
Granger, IN 46530

www.liveyourjoy.org

It is with deep love that I dedicate this book to my daughter, Kim Gulbranson, an extraordinarily kind, wise, and inspirational woman who follows her dreams and her heart. I am eternally grateful and blessed to share life, laughter and love with her on this planet.

Lord, make me an instrument of thy peace.
Where there is hatred, let me sow love;
Where there is injury, pardon;
Where there is doubt, faith;
Where there is despair, hope;
Where there is darkness, light;
Where there is sadness, joy.

Oh divine Master, grant
that I may not so much seek
To be consoled as to console,
To be understood as to understand,
To be loved as to love;
For it is in giving that we receive;
It is in pardoning that we are pardoned;
It is in dying [to self] that we are born to eternal life.

— SAINT FRANCES OF ASSISI

Contents

Introduction xv

1: Focus on Kindness 1
The Open Heart 5
The Benefits of Kindness 6
Kindness in Action 9

2: Experience the Miracle of Oneness 15
Living in Nonduality 21
A Oneness Lesson from a Bunny 23
Practicing Universal Love 26
Kindness in Action 27

3: Access the Healing Power of Kindness 31
A Sacred Space 34
Spiritual Bypasses 35
Kindness Heals 41
Grief's Silver Lining 42
Kindness in Action 45

4: Be a Little Kind to Your Self 51
Busting Cultural Myths 54
From Powerless to Empowerment 56
Practicing Self-Kindness 58
Kindness in Action 61

5: Get Your Attitude On 65
A Bodhichitta Thing 68
A Better World 71
Kindness in Action 74

6: Bask in the Joy of Forgiveness 79
Doorway to Freedom 83
A Forgiveness Practice 84
Kindness in Action 86

7: Survive the Terrible Twos 93
The Face of Fear 94
Out of Fear 97
Working with Anger 99
Kindness in Action 103

8: Cultivate Kindness 105
Egolessness 106
Equanimity 109
Generosity 114
A Wall of Gratitude 119
Kindness in Action 121

9: Relax into the Simplicity of Being 125
Back to Basics 128
Not for Mystics Only 131
Mother Meditation 139
Centering Prayer 140
Lovingkindness Meditation 141
Kriya Yoga 146
Pure Land Buddhist Meditation 147
Transcendental Meditation (TM) 149

Bliss Revealed 150
Kindness in Action 151

10: Empty the Trash 155
The Beauty of Kenosis 157
Making Room for God 161
Kindness in Action 167

11: Awaken to Your World of Transformation 171

APPENDICES
Appendix One—Developing Bodhichitta Attitude 175
Appendix Two—Your Kindness Tool Kit 179
Appendix Three—What Authentic Kindness Feels Like 181
Appendix Four—An Exploration of Oneness 183
Appendix Five—The Art of Forgiving 185
Appendix Six—New Thinking Patterns 187
Appendix Seven—Taking the Vow 191

Introduction

The human condition is one of suffering. Poverty, pain, crime, famine, and incurable illness touch our lives and those around us. Every time we turn on the news or search the Internet, we see images of bombings, shootings, and natural disasters. It seems as if our world is spiraling out of control. In the midst of turmoil, we crave lasting peace and joy, which seem to be out of reach or just a pipe dream at best. We long for a more peaceful and loving society but don't find happiness in the accumulation of wealth or material possessions. Nor do we find happiness in the pursuit of sensory pleasure, or in acquiring the next electronic gizmo that eats up much of our time. There is, however, a practical path to peace, love, and joy for us and the rest of civilization—a path that everyone can walk to not only help navigate through challenging times but to bring life blessings beyond measure.

The path I am talking about is the path of authentic kindness. It's up to us to plant the seeds of compassion to make radical change in our world. When we offer authentic kindness to others, we help alleviate the suffering of humanity and promote transformation and awakening in humankind. We give kindness to others in an organic way without asking or expecting anything in return. Kindness, in its purest form, is transformational. Just one drop of kindness is transformative for the individual and society. Expressions of authentic kindness are different from when we might act kind because we have to or because we want to make a good impression. They are different from acts of kindness performed to get something in return. They are different from "good acts" we think might elicit good karma, praise, or favor with God. In expressions of authentic kindness, we give—and experience—love and compassion in a deeper way... a way that comes from the core of our being.

Authentic kindness arises from a natural urge in our hearts to help others. It comes from recognizing that all of creation is interconnected. We understand that other people are fundamentally like us—they have the same feelings, needs, and fears that we do. There is no separation from God to humans, humans to humans, and God to animals. Coming from this nondual or unitive consciousness allows us to open our hearts and experience authentic kindness that radiates out to others, touches their hearts, and relieves their suffering. As a result of remembering our shared humanity, we are able to extend authentic kindness not only to those we love, but also to those who have harmed us as well. This is the deepest form of compassion, a compassion that heals us as individuals and as a society.

Every day presents opportunities to practice authentic kindness. Whenever we come in contact with another person, there is an opportunity to share your light and love with the world. Whenever we witness, for example, a frenzied sales associate bagging groceries, a burdened waitress juggling trays, or a weary computer repair person facing a long line of disgruntled customers, we have openings to transform the moment by sharing kindness. Frequently, I saw this type of altruistic kindness when I worked as a hospice chaplain and most recently in my position as the director of the Suicide Prevention Center. A caregiver or family member extends a comforting touch, a gentle wipe of the brow, or a warm smile.

Within each one of us is a source of happiness that everyone can access even during the most difficult times. We can connect with the sacred and loving aspect of the Divine through authentic kindness. From the compassionate heart, we bring the Divine out in the open, and we act as an instrument of the universe. Not only is the one whom you gifted an act of kindness made happier, you are also uplifted uplifted and transformed by serving as an agent of Spirit. Kindness works that way. The more you give it away, the more you get in terms of love, peace, and joy. However, your kindness must be authentic.

Love and kindness go hand and hand; they cannot be separated. One of the ways you know you are giving authentic kindness is in your automatic response. When you feel the wide expanse of love in your heart during the exchange, authentic kindness—and the Divine—are present within you. We shift from living from the vantage point of the "self" to the living to serve others. Spreading loving energy brings spiritual awakening to all humanity—an awakening that is urgently needed in our turbulent world.

Anyone can live healthy in the self and be in service to others at the same time. We should not forget self-care, which is especially important to make us better vehicles for serving, but we must make some changes to shift our focus toward serving others with authentic kindness naturally and continuously. While serving doesn't mean we should develop a serious nature or renounce our own connection with others, we must drop the ego and shift the focus on "I" to focus on the world. An outward focus is the deep spiritual calling we are all meant to express. While how we carry out our life's purpose is different for each of us depending on our spiritual gifts and what we came here to do, we all have opportunities to serve no matter what walk of life we are in. We each share the calling to love and live for others.

Living with a commitment to service doesn't mean we live devoid of joy. It's in the giving that we receive the most joy and can conduct our lives with good humor, gratitude, and a "how can I serve today?" attitude. We don't have to renounce our jobs, our lifestyle, or our families to do so. In serving, we are practicing a powerful form of kindness which melts the frozen heart and opens an avenue for love deeper than anything we have known before. By strengthening this type of genuine kindness in our hearts, we can change people's lives and ultimately the entire planet. Think of serving as part of an advanced spiritual practice. Some of the most advanced spiritual practices are the easiest to understand and most effortless ones to incorporate into our daily lives.

Once we sow the seeds of authentic kindness, we can no longer be selfish, unloving, egotistical, critical or judgmental. Negative traits simply melt away when we steep the heart in God's love and extend this love out to others. You don't have to search for this kindness because it is already woven into your being. Lovingkindness is a quality of God that is already within us, waiting for full expression. The key to unleashing the unbounded love of God is to practice this deep, sacred kindness. Humanity is crying out to receive this type of love; it's up to us to answer the holy call to action. Opportunities to give love and kindness abound everywhere in everyday life. We must look for them, find our agency in extending ourselves meaningfully in service, and call upon our innate compassion. Our rewards will be great. The Dalai Lama tells us, "When we feel love and kindness toward others, it not only makes others feel loved and cared for, but it helps us also to develop inner happiness and peace."

Our compassion also lifts us to higher levels of consciousness. A heart basked in love and kindness is the most beautiful and precious gift to ourselves and the world. Because the heart is the organ—physically or metaphorically—through which spiritual perception takes place, cultivating a kind and loving heart is the path to personal transformation. When we have this unbounded love for God and all of creation (including the animal kingdom and the environment), we attain the Infinite Bliss mode of action.[1] The Infinite Bliss mode of action is a state of bliss consciousness exhibiting a complete union with the Divine. This is where the human is completely immersed in God, living in a state of gratitude and having shed the ego completely. In this highest level of consciousness, we remain even-minded and untouched by anything unlike love. Yes, we are still faced with challenges like anyone else, but even in the midst of our bleakest experiences, we internally transcend the challenges, gain mental perspective of the situation, and stay emotionally rooted in love and kindness. From this peaceful place in our souls, we arrive at a vibratory state where the light of the Divine within intensifies. While this exquisite light can grow dim from stress, pain, and negativity, it can never be severed from you. It is the eternal flame of Spirit alive in each one of us.

In this high place of awareness, we become fully awakened and self-actualized human beings who don't give out kindness mechanically but from the fullness of our hearts giving and seeking nothing in return. Our kindness is transformed from a "what can I get from this" attitude to an overflowing river of selfless generosity. Now we stand as a humble, naked, and gentle agent of God on Earth. For me, I begin the day with a prayer affirming that Spirit use me as its instrument to bring guidance, love, and blessings to those I meet. This sets the tone for the day and I feel wide expansion in my heart from being a willing and humble servant of Spirit.

To cultivate authentic kindness, we must shed any hard shell that we might be using as protection. We discard the mantle of hard-heartedness, no matter what anyone has done to hurt us intentionally or unintentionally. The very act of discarding our emotional armor brings deep compassion and unbounded joy. We entrust our affairs to Spirit and, in return, are released from the clutches of anything unlike love and kindness so our soft, gentle and tender side predominates our existence. Life's struggles can then make us more understanding and kind; they can actually become a source of renewed strength and radiant beauty. When we clear away the weeds that strangle our capacity for authentic kindness, our heart becomes wide open for the living Presence of God, which is always within us. This is the moment that our awakening takes place.

The goal of this book is to inspire everyone to extend kindness out toward all of creation, eliminate cruelty, develop egolessness in the individual, and encourage people to live and love from the magnificent holy place within. This book draws from many faith traditions. Some of these teachings may resonate with you; others may not. Take what feels true in your heart and soul and embody those sacred principles in your life. Most importantly, you don't have to practice any particular religion to apply these practices in your life; they are universal and for everyone alike.

As a reader of a book like this one, you are already a kind and loving person. Now let's go a little deeper and become more sensitive and vulnerable. Let's open the door to emptying ourselves of anything unlike kindness and let our hearts be bathed in the warm glow of love that comes from being a selfless servant of Spirit. Start your day by volunteering to be an instrument of the Divine. Let the light of God shine bright and strong out from your heart to others. Step into the glory of giving authentic kindness. This, then, is our spiritual prescription: to heal the hearts of humanity—to love, to be kind, and to be the light on earth. Let's answer the sacred calling to uplift the world and those who live in it through authentic kindness.

Chapter One

Focus on Kindness

"The simplest acts of kindness are far more powerful than a thousand heads bowing in prayer."

— MAHATMA GANDHI

Authentic kindness springs from a heart that is steeped in love. As a result of authentic kindness, the Divine Presence and the human soul touch in such a sacred way that love automatically pours out from one heart to another. Authentic kindness goes beyond empathy and represents an active longing to obliterate the suffering of others. Its very essence is love and compassion. At the core of this type of kindness is selflessness. Rather than focusing on ourselves, we want to end the suffering of others and help them live joyously.

As you can see, authentic kindness is much more than performing a "random act of kindness," which is defined as an unexpected and unearned good deed done for someone we may or may not know, although that has merit of its own; it is unconditional love in full bloom, in its purest form. Authentic kindness is different from obligatory kindness, like when a child shares a toy because her parents say she must, or when an adult brings a gift to a party because it is expected. A random act of kindness or gesture of obligatory kindness may be authentic, the concepts are not necessarily mutually exclusive. However, unlike a surface gesture of pay it forward or contrived type of kindness, expressions of authentic kindness represent a much deeper experience because they come from a Divine Source within ourselves that transcends humanness and longs to be a vessel of compassion for others. Authentic kindness represents unadulterated love untainted by judgment, criticism, jealousy, aggressiveness, greed and ego.

Ego-consciousness and authentic kindness cannot coexist because the ego is the basis of duality—making you feel like you are separate from God—and from this belief system, authentic kindness cannot grow. The dichotomy is why dropping the ego's stronghold is so important, first for your own well-being and second for the well-being of everyone around you. Authentic kindness cannot exist in the lower levels of consciousness because those levels are filled with fear, ego, selfishness, anger, jealousy, and drama. Kind inclinations develop naturally when one reaches the higher states of consciousness, which are marked by love, peace, joy, compassion, even-mindedness, empathy, and stillness.

Practicing authentic kindness frees us from negativity and limiting beliefs and puts us on the path to peace, love, and joy. Being kind naturally occurs from a heart filled with love and compassion and an intense desire to alleviate world suffering. Each drop of kindness we give multiplies to an ocean of kindness in which the depths are boundless. Giving kindness from the inside out transforms us into faithful instruments of the Divine and true agents of change in our world. We radiate joy and see unlimited opportunities to give love and compassion to others. In this enthusiastic feeling that results from the outpouring of love comes a stillness and peace within. We become deeply connected with God and go about our lives joyfully living to serve and helping to heal the lives of others.

When practicing authentic kindness, the goal is not to have a life devoid of suffering, because suffering is part of the human condition, but to offer solace and compassion to those who are experiencing suffering. By simply remembering our shared humanity, we are able to give authentic kindness not only to those we love, but also to those who have hurt us as well. This is the deepest form of compassion, and it is this compassion that heals us as individuals and as a society.

We all have the innate ability to love and help those in need. Sadly, for many of us expressions of love are reserved only for those with whom we have personal relationships. After all, it is easy to be kind to those we love. But what about people we don't have relationships with or those who push our buttons? Is it just as easy to be kind to them? This is when things get sticky for us. How do we extend this love and compassion out from our inner circle to the rest of the world? It can be done with simple spiritual practices such as self-emptying and meditation that we will explore in this book. When you have cultivated the art of kindness from deep in the heart, love spans all of creation and is not confined to people of our choosing. Our world today is crying out for us to have a kind heart, not only to those we love, but to those who are outside of the perimeter of our relationship sphere, even to those who have done us harm.

What may be surprising to some people is that when giving kindness, it is the giver who is rewarded with deep abiding peace and unbounded joy. When I worked as a hospice chaplain, I experienced this often and saw it taking place all around me. If I came to work with personal challenges and held the hand of a dying patient, offering comfort and compassion, my personal issues melted away and the Divine in my soul merged with the Divine in the other person.

It turns out that giving kindness and compassion to a patient or, in my current work, to a suicide survivor or one contemplating suicide, makes my heart swell with love and connects with the other person in the deepest, almost magical, way. I saw this especially in the aides, nurses, doctors, and loved ones caring for people with Alzheimer's disease, cancer, heart disease, and other terminal illnesses. The smallest of gestures sometimes seem to have the greatest value for the patient. In these circumstances, we can see how the simple act of loving is so healing to one's entire being, whether we are the giver or the receiver. This is unconditional love—giving love without asking for or seeking anything in return. Yet the return is great in terms of love and spiritual development; it creates a deepening of the connection with the spiritual aspect in each one of us. Giving authentic kindness creates a wonderful feeling inside and comes from our oneness of being—the Divine within you connecting with the Divine within another. Even greater, expressions of authentic kindness produce a ripple effect; those who receive it want to give it, and as a result it multiplies and touches the hearts of many.

The Open Heart

One of the keys to cultivating authentic kindness is to open your heart. Opening your heart completely without protecting or shielding it in any way is a major step in expanding kindness and compassion. Opening your heart is also the way to spiritual progress and growth. Having an open heart sets the groundwork for authentic kindness, whereas holding onto resentments, hurts, judgments, and grudges blocks you from developing this beautiful quality. Becoming a humble and egoless person opens your heart further to welcome in kindness. Being humble does not mean being weak; rather, it is understanding that I do nothing myself and "the Father within me does the work." Recognizing that God is the actor behind all kindness is humbling because we are acknowledging that we are acting not as humans but as instruments of God. To develop this type of attitude requires a still mind. If we keep ourselves on overload, always busy and doing, we become stressed and don't readily feel connected with the Divine Presence within. Kindness comes from that still place within, that harmony with all of life. It's an at-one-ment with all of creation.

Opening our hearts transforms our lives in so many ways. Not only do we become a vehicle of kindness in the world, but our personal lives get better through harmonious, loving relationships, gratitude, and inner peace. We no longer have the inclination to judge or criticize others. We develop a deep-seated patience for others and discover that everyone is operating from their own level of consciousness and cannot operate from any other place. This allows us to feel compassion and empathy toward others. We drop the need to be right or to prove our point and can instead lovingly meet and accept people where they are on their sacred paths. Additionally, we lose the need to control others or the outcome of any situation.

Authentic kindness yields all these positive outcomes and so much more. We have a choice to make. We can choose to be kind and to experience unparalleled levels of joy, or to be engulfed by our egos and to experience the misery that ego consciousness brings. Choosing the path of authentic kindness is one that offers a double blessing—a blessing for the one who gives kindness and a blessing for the one who receives it.

The Benefits of Kindness

Research indicates that one of the best ways to boost your own happiness is by rendering kindness to others and enhancing other people's happiness. Studies have found that kindness and generosity may be linked to greater life satisfaction and stronger relationships as well as better mental and physical health. According to many studies, kind people may actually live longer; some scientists say that kind people age two times slower than most of the population. The reason may be found partially in the research that explores the physiological processes. Some studies suggest people who are consistently kind may have lower levels of cortisol, which is the hormone that increases with emotional stress. Other research indicates that feeling kindness produces endorphins, which elevate happiness and are the brain's natural painkillers. The physical advantages are found in those giving and receiving kindness.

Even though numerous studies show the health benefits of kindness, we give authentic kindness freely without thinking about what is in it for ourselves. We are not kind with a motive of living a longer life or getting healthier. For some people, remembering the health benefits may be a good starting point in developing authentic kindness, and we should start wherever we are. But more important than health benefits, kindness results in spiritual growth in terms of greater joy, life satisfaction, deepening connection with God, and inner peace. The natural workings of universal law dictate that the energy we exude goes out into the universe and attracts like energy back to us. When we emit the energy of love through kindness, we receive love and kindness in return.

Daily kindness is the root of happiness in life and the answer to human suffering. To grow the seeds of kindness in your heart, wake up in the morning and pray:

Dear God, use me as your instrument today to give compassion, love, and kindness to everyone I meet. I offer myself as your humble servant and I serve with a smile on my face and joy in my heart.

Say this simple prayer and see how your life is transformed in glorious ways. As his Holiness the Dalai Lama said, "There is no need for temples; no need for complicated philosophy. Our own brain, our own heart is our temple; the philosophy is kindness." We can view our society as heartless and brutal or we can recognize that it is also filled with love, kindness, and compassion. We can recognize that when we see tragic events in the world, they typically elicit an outpouring of love and compassion that strengthens a bond across humanity. Interestingly, suicide rates drop when there is a world tragedy as people band together and feel an increased sense of connectedness. This was clearly seen during the World Trade Center terrorist attacks when the suicide rates in the United States for September 11, 2001, decreased by more than 60 percent of the typical daily rate of deaths by suicide. This was the lowest daily rate ever in the history of the country.

With this sense of connectedness in our hearts at all times, we can be the ones to herald in a new age of kindness by dropping our negative patterns such as limiting beliefs, fear, guilt, shame, aggression, judgment and criticism, and becoming of service to humanity while lighting the way for others to follow in our sacred footsteps.

Whatever the unique gifts that you bring to the world, there's one thing we all share in common and that is the capacity to give love and compassion to others. Living from the vantage point of being of service to God, the world brings us gifts beyond measure. Here's an example from my own life.

I was visiting a ninety-nine-year-old hospice patient suffering from Alzheimer's disease. At the close of our visit, I asked if I could give her a hug. She said, "Why not? And may you have nice things happen to you all day long." You see, while I thought I was the one rendering kindness, it was me who actually received the blessing. May you, too, dear reader, have nice things happen to you all day long.

Kindness in Action

One organization that clearly demonstrates the benefits of kindness on the individual and the world is U R Awesome Inc., a nonprofit organization that helps youth discover and actualize their potential to be kind while empowering them to meaningfully serve others. You may be aware of this organization's initiatives to give "free hugs" in the public or by national media coverage of founder Kemy Joseph's talks and positive mission. The organization's Kindness Coaching programs are interactive community-building presentations that empower students to rise above bullying by creating school environments that foster acceptance and collaboration. When students are asked at the beginning of the program what stops them from being kind, many report they are depressed and afraid of being made fun of by their classmates. During the kindness programs, many high school students start baring their souls. The response from other student participants can be life-changing for everyone involved. In one program, for example, a student who was dealing with mental challenges shared how others in the program had stepped forward to help him get to class and help him with homework. The students in the program, when they heard how his life had changed for the better, cheered and applauded. Everyone was blessed and encouraged as witnesses of the transformative power of kindness.

According to Kemy Joseph, MS, EDS, "Everyone is awesome; everyone is connected. When we can help people remember that they can be kind and empathic." Kemy's own kind heart sprang from cruelty. He grew up in a strict home with spanking punishment which fueled his fire to physically attack and beat his peers. He bullied and stole from others, thinking there was no other way to survive. As a result of his cruel actions, he landed in the corrections system and was arrested twice. Kemy explains that this was his "wake-up call." Although he then straightened up his behavior, Kemy continued to live in scarcity mode, believing his resources would always be limited so he should grab what he could. Then his dad was later hit and killed by a drunk driver when Kemy was age fourteen, and everything changed... including Kemy's outlook. He realized the world was not about the individual self and there were many more dimensions at play. He realized his unkind ways would only lead to pain and suffering for himself and others, as they always had. The universe showed his actions had a negative impact; yet, by grace, many people such as teachers and athletic coaches supported Kemy and his family. The trauma opened his eyes to recognize the support and love from other people. If his eyes weren't open, he could have gone down a different path. The awareness then came of how more positive ways by him could multiply kindness.

As a result of the love and support Kemy received, he was able to succeed in school to achieve a full college scholarship. In college, he wore signs on his chest with positive messages such as "You are awesome," "Spreading love and peace," and "Love who you are." This was the first time he stood out for kindness. His approach gave him unique first-hand witness to how an individual's intentional, positive actions can affect people directly in the moment. Their reactions were sometimes surprising. Kemy observed, "Some people have been through worse and show up positive and full of love."

Kemy states, "Kindness reminds us that we are awesome and have this power to impact ourselves and the world being able to see how I can make an impact on someone's life." He's seen people change and this shows the true power that we have—to make the world a better place by exercising their positive power. Another benefit of kindness, he adds, is "on the psychological level because endorphins and serotonin are released that help us relax and live longer because the body is releasing positive chemicals."

The biggest challenge to people's self-actualization, or becoming all that a human being can be, is that people get a preponderance of erroneous societal messages that indicate they are unworthy, the world is unsafe, and kindness is a sign of weakness. This is why it takes effort from us to convince others that kindness is a stronger power than being a bully; we have to break through the muck of wrong thinking.

Kemy said he used to feel rejected if someone turned down a kind act, but he has faith in the bigger picture than in the individual. He believes, "Even if nothing comes out of my kindness with you… the kindness I'm putting out will come around." Kindness, even if it is rejected, isn't wasted because we have to look at the bigger picture. Eventually, kindness that people receive will motivate them to extend kindness. Kemy expresses heartfelt thanks to those who helped him learn these life lessons which he believes are crucial. He says, "It's becoming more and more evident that kindness can save people's lives."

Affirmation

I am an awesome and worthy child of God. Joyfully I extend kindness to myself and others.

Chapter Two

Experience the Miracle of Oneness

"We have to take the whole universe as the expression of the one Self. Then only our love flows to all beings and creatures in the world equally."

— SWAMI RAMDAS

Love and kindness bring us happiness far greater than anything else because expressions and feelings give us an opening to touch each other's hearts as spiritual beings. The reason we are able to connect with others through love is in the unity we share—the oneness of all creation. For the God within me is the same God within you; and each time we give even one drop of love, it is recognized by the other. So, then, the secret to happiness is simply this: give unceasingly to others without expecting anything in return. By alleviating the suffering of others through expressing kindness, the path to your happiness will be made clear before you.

Authentic kindness, that which is borne by love, comes from not only realizing but experiencing the deep feeling and knowing that we are all connected—we are all part of the one source, the one heart, the one life, which is God. Realizing the interconnectedness of all living beings is the key to obliterating crime, corruption, and war. Interconnectedness is what allows kindness, love, and compassion that bursts from deep within our hearts to touch others in a most intimate way. This is what Jesus was talking about when he said each of us should love our neighbor as ourself. He was talking about recognizing your neighbor as an aspect of yourself. Paramahansa Yoganada, an Indian yogi and guru who introduced many Westerners to the teachings of Kriya Yoga, said, "Man has hypnotized himself into thinking that he is a human being, whereas in reality he is one with God." This is what's called nondual, or unitive, consciousness—no separation between God and all of creation, including humans and the animal kingdom.

This basic principle, that God is oneness manifesting itself through all of creation, means that God is in all and through all, making each of us aspects of the one life, one heart, one mind. You can call it whatever you want: Spirit, God, Creator, the Infinite, Atman, Brahman, Buddha, Jehovah, Elohim or Yahweh, but there is no doubt that a Divine Presence is the spark of life in each one of us—the animal kingdom, the ocean kingdom, and the nature world—all of life. St. Francis recognized this oneness and called the animals (as well as the universe, Sun, Moon and all of nature) brothers. Coming from this nondual consciousness opens our hearts in an almost magical way, allowing us to have authentic kindness from within that extends out to all of creation. A transformation takes place, and we operate on a whole new level of consciousness.

Authentic Kindness

The principle of oneness is an important part of spiritual transformation because we cannot give kindness and compassion in totality until we recognize the oneness of each and honor all of creation. Everything is linked to each other on this planet. For example, when you read or watch the news and hear about a murder, crime or abuse, you feel sadness. That is only possible because we are all interconnected with that same something, that same common thread of the Divine within us. When you see and revere the Divine in your own being, then you can see it in other people and animals, too. Recognizing this spiritual aspect in all of life allows you to release judgment and criticism, and compassion begins to flow from you. You don't ask if others are worthy or deserving of your compassion. Since they are as one with the light of God innately in them (just like it is in you), they are inherently worthy of love and compassion, no matter what the outer appearance. The unearthing of a deep feeling of interconnectedness is quite a relief because now you are on a path of spiritual growth that can transform your life from a material plane, with all of its neuroses, to living on a spiritual plane where love, kindness, and compassion are the natural outcomes of a heart infused with unconditional love.

One of the most beautiful explanations of oneness is when Jesus says, "I" am in God, God is in you, you are in God, we are in each other. His teaching in John 15 in the Christian Bible clearly shows the unity between God and creation. He says, "I am the vine; you are the branches. Abide in me as I in you." This awareness of the oneness of life is also at the core of New Thought teachings which explain the teachings of Jesus further, stating that the manifest universe is the body of God and is the outcome of self-knowingness of God. God is through all and is ALL—omniscient, omnipresent, and omnipotent.

By contrast, people who live in the world with a dual mentality are in the lower modes of consciousness. They see the worst in others and themselves, and operate out of fear, judgment, and negativity. Not knowing that Spirit is alive within them, they go around with a "poor me" or "what's in it for me" attitude. Aggression felt and expressed as fear, greed, judgment, self-centeredness, gossip, and clinging are predominant in their lives. Such a state of awareness is what I call Drama Dance.[1] It is a lower state of consciousness where the individual is struggling and going about life unfulfilled, believing that he or she is a victim of circumstance or at the mercy of random acts. Drama Dance people accept false beliefs and live according to a sensory world of earthly pleasure, pain, and disappointment. Unsatisfying relationships, economic hardship, ill health, stress, and anxiety are prevalent here. These people feel totally separate from one another and grasp at whatever material item or sensory pleasure will satisfy a longing for happiness.

With feelings of helplessness, depression, victimization, and unworthiness, life seems to be a continuing drama of tragedy, sorrow, and misfortune. This person may be prone to substance abuse, poor interpersonal relationships, unemployment, and financial disaster. There is a feeling of separateness from God and little hope for a bright future.

It's like a drug addict who keeps consuming drugs, but never can satisfy the longing within; there is always a craving for more. Craving things cannot bring happiness because, even if momentarily satisfied, the satisfaction is fleeting. Holding on to false pleasure, those in the Drama Dance mode of consciousness cling to satisfying their cravings like their lives depend on it. The cravings—physical, mental, or emotional—represent searching for something more and yet that something is right within us at all times, as we are one with our Creator and can never be separated from it. Peace and happiness cannot arise from dual consciousness.

Fortunately, we can grow out of dual consciousness by taking heed of two things Jesus said that exemplify the oneness of all. He said, "The Father and I are one," and "Love your neighbor as yourself." If Jesus and the Father are one, that means we, too, are one with the Father. We are not the whole but we are aspects of the whole, and divinity lives within each one of us. Likewise, when Jesus said, "Love your neighbor as yourself," he was instructing us to see our neighbors as an extension of ourselves because we are all parts of the whole, which is God. When we come to see our neighbors as the face of God, we open our hearts to love and compassion.

An example of seeing our neighbors as the face of God took place one Holy Thursday when a group of ministers from different faiths participated in a moving and emotional foot washing of women janitors in San Diego, California. The event was sponsored by the Interfaith Center for Social Justice and several other nonprofit service organizations. It began as a powerful march by many janitors and supporters. One janitor carried a huge wooden cross as they walked several blocks to the downtown Civic Center Plaza singing songs such as "Amazing Grace" and "Here We Are, Lord." The women janitors told heart-wrenching stories about the injustices they endured while on the job such as: low wages, sexual harassments, exploitation, and the rape of female janitors. Remembering how Jesus washed the feet of his disciples as a way to role model humility and service to others, the supporters were there that day to follow his way and be in humble service to the janitors and their plight. Various faith leaders from the Roman Catholic tradition and the Islamic tradition, as well as spiritual leaders from the Episcopal, Unitarian Universalists, Quakers, and other denominations, spoke to express their support and bless the women. Then the clergy and those who wanted to participate were invited to wash the feet of the janitors. One minister, Rev. Abigail Albert, washed the feel of an older lady. Rev. Albert said, "I just kept looking into her eyes and I talked and I felt the beauty of her soul, the sweetness of her countenance. I saw the face of God." Tears sprung up in the janitor's eyes and she said, according to Rev. Albert, "You are a very kind lady." This was love and authentic kindness in action–a powerful testimonial to the beautiful outcome of feeling and honoring the oneness of all.

Living in Nonduality

We shift our perspective from a dualistic point of view to a nondualistic one by going beyond understanding the concept of the interconnectedness of all to feeling the connection deeply in our beings and living from this space in our hearts. Then our interactions with others become sacred acts of love and compassion. If everyone lived in this manner, the possibilities for societal healing would be boundless. Crime would melt away in the world and greed, corruption, and misuse of our natural resources would be forever vanquished.

As individuals living from this calm center, we enter the kingdom of heaven on earth and find ourselves in the Divine flow of life. The treasure within us, which is our inherent divinity, lies latent within us, waiting for us to discover it and use it to add to the light of the world. When we discover the Spirit within, duality consciousness is shed and we no longer see ourselves as singular individuals out for our own gain. We are transformed into seeing the divinity in all and through all, and honoring this knowledge in every interaction that we have with humans, animals, and nature. Discovering the oneness of all and seeing through the eyes of God is something everyone can do, it's not just for saints and sages, or mystics and gurus. This is a natural path that everyone can walk without special skills or training. However, no one can do this for us; we must discover it for ourselves.

Living in nonduality brings us peace and respite in our own hearts and opens us to giving unbounded compassion and kindness to others. How can we possibly be unkind when everyone we meet is an expression of the One? Knowing that we are aspects of God is what lifts our lives to greater meaning. We move out of human consciousness and step into the realm of spiritual consciousness. We no longer seek refuge in the outer world of sensory pleasures, but find our greatest pleasure comes from expressing the living Spirit within. While we appreciate the outer world, we go deeper and embrace all aspects of our being. We live in the Divine flow and know ourselves as the spiritual beings that we are.

In the *Gospel of Thomas*, Jesus said:

> *"When you know yourself, then you will be known,*
> *And you will know that you are the child of the Living Father;*
> *But if you do not know yourself,*
> *you will live in vain*
> *and you will be vanity."*

This remembrance that we are all children of the Living Father—that divinity lives within each and every one of us—gives us the power to love one another and appreciate the many aspects of God within. The remembrance prompts us to extend kindness and compassion in a way that transcends suffering and pain, and enables us to radiate love and light to everyone we meet. A nondualistic nature nurtures a tenderness in our hearts that grows. Love automatically springs from our hearts and we feel deep love and compassion for other beings. It is precisely because of our interconnectedness with all of creation that we feel so good when we are in service to others. Research shows that feeling this connection to others satisfies a basic psychological need to belong; when the need is met, people are more likely to care for others. Conversely, when the need for belongingness is not met, people focus more on their own needs than other people's needs. Interestingly, "thwarted belongingness" is a serious risk factor for suicide. When someone feels like he or she no longer belongs and does not feel connected with others, the person's risk of death by suicide increases.

Achieving a holy state where we recognize and revere the oneness of all takes more than understanding; it takes direct experience. Your connection to the Divine always exists as does your neighbors' connection. The Divine is truly in every aspect of life, drop of the ocean, blade of grass, person, and animal that walks the earth. But sometimes we forget who we are: that we are children of God—part of the one life, one heart, one presence. For a moment, picture in your mind what it would be like if you could feel holistic interconnectedness as you went about your daily life. How would your day be different? How would your interactions with people soften? What would it feel like if you lived, moved, and breathed from the vantage point of oneness with all of creation? How would your choices regarding, for example, treatment of animals change?

A Oneness Lesson from a Bunny

When I was eight years old, my grandfather, who was an avid hunter, kept bunnies in pens on his country property. Whenever my family visited him, I was overjoyed to play with the adorable bunnies. I even named one of my favorites Snowflake. Snowflake had beautiful white fur, but what drew me to him was his sweet disposition; he was affectionate, eager, and trusting. I enjoyed feeding him bits of vegetables from my hands, which he gently took while I held him. The next time I visited my grandparents' country home, I ran out to the pen to see Snowflake as soon as I could break away from the family. I knew I would recognize Snowflake's distinctive colorings from the dozens of bunnies in the pens and searched in vain to find my furry friend. I didn't know what happened to him—just that he was gone. My grandmother's huge Italian dinner with pasta, gravy, and all the fixings that night was consolation while I wondered and worried about Snowflake. I loved my grandmother and everyone adored her comfort food. You can therefore imagine my horror and deep feeling of betrayal when I learned later in the evening that my beloved Snowflake's carcass was in the gravy.

My stomach roiled and my eyes burned with tears. I cried, "How could Grandpa have killed Snowflake?" I lamented, "How could Grandma cook Snowflake for dinner?" I searched deep in my soul and could not answer these questions. But what I did find was a deep reverence for all of life. For me, this was a turning point—the ultimate realization of the unity of all of life. Snowflake taught me that all of life is one and when we harm any part of life, we harm ourselves. People sometimes quote certain Bible passages or say, "Well, we have dominion over animals." Our dominion, or our control by virtue of superior cunning, does not mean we have the right to kill those who cannot compete. Our dominion means merely that we have the faculty of reason that animals don't have, an opportunity to think and plan, to see the long view. Our faculty of reason should be used to honor the interconnectedness of all of life. As the Buddha once said, "The eating of meat extinguishes the seed of great compassion." And Zen Master Thich Thanh Tu said, "Being a vegetarian makes it easier for us to increase our loving kindness and compassion."

Please don't misunderstand: it's not my intention to admonish or judge those who eat meat. I, too, was brought up in a home where meat was served and I ate it. What I am suggesting is that we need to raise our consciousness level. In seeking oneness, we must not overlook the values that society instills in us, but instead evaluate for ourselves the inconsistencies that arise in our awakened souls. We should be aware of everything we take within us—food, air, light, warmth, and so forth. One element of enlightenment is to be conscious of what, exactly, we are eating and where it came from. In knowledge and awareness, we then can fully decide what to ingest. We may decide to avoid meat and/or a whole host of other substances. The decision is ours. In proper awareness, we may say a prayer before meals for that which we are about to take in and, if applicable, thank the animal for sacrificing its life.

Barbara Gulbranson

Practicing Universal Love

What is called for today is a need to honor all of creation and a demonstration of universal love for all. To remind yourself of the connectedness of life, affirm to yourself:

*I see, feel, and sense my oneness with all of creation.
I honor the divinity within all and allow the full
expression of God to express through me as gentleness,
love, and compassion this day and always.*

Then simply go about your day and see what happens. Be aware of the oneness of all and let the joy of this understanding wash over you. There may be moments when you forget, but gently bring your mind back to the affirmation above. I assure you that you will feel an expanse in your heart and have experiences of harmony and beauty. Your heart will swell with love because you are a breeding ground for compassion and kindness. It's a blissful way to live and you can do it on a daily basis for the rest of your life. In these beautiful moments of honoring the oneness of all, when you really feel the Divine permeating all of life, you will feel joy like never before. Cherish this spiritual transformation and your awakened heart. Once you feel this sacred connection, it will spread like wildfire within yourself and out to every heart you touch during your daily life. You will be richly blessed with the awareness of the oneness of being. This, then, is one of the keys to authentic kindness. It's a magical key that you hold in your heart always and forevermore.

Kindness in Action

She sits at an animal sanctuary in Mapoli, Maharashtra, India, and hears the howling and crying of a dog, and then a loud thud. The howling and crying begins again, and then the thud. She looks over at the cages of the dogs. One dog is climbing its cage wall, howling and crying, then falls to the floor, defeated. Thud. Repeat. She sees and feels the crazy frenzy, the loneliness, the painful cry for love and freedom.

Rev. MyShell Howler, also known as Ahowan ICrow, is an ordained animal chaplain (OAC) and president, spiritual leader, and cofounder of AHOWAN Traveling Spiritual Sanctuary. She shares with us one of her experiences as an OAC who travels the world helping animals and honoring the oneness of life by administering love and kindness to all of creation. She continues to relate her experience in the Mapoli sanctuary. She says she next hears one of the workers yell the dog's name, shake his head, smile at her, then speak to the other worker. Pointing at the dog, they laugh.

Goldie is the name of the lonely, crazed dog. Along with the other dogs, Goldie has been locked up for months. MyShell watches the feeding process and routines of each day, observing that the dogs do not get even a touch from a hand; they receive only "food, water, and a brief cleaning of their cage." One day, MyShell walks over to Goldie with some kibble in her hand and gives a few minutes of intense petting and eye gazing. MyShell says, "I can feel the [dog's] gratitude of being recognized, loved, and mostly, being touched."

Upon closing the cage door, MyShell relates, Goldie walks to the back of the cage, curls up in a ball, and falls asleep, content for now.

MyShell concludes, "It only takes a few minutes to offer a loving gesture that makes one feel loved, acknowledged, and peaceful. It means more than food, water, or cleanliness... these can be given without love or a heart. But to extend your heart through your hand and offer a loving touch can heal and be more kind than anything else in this world."

Affirmation

I make conscious choices about how I nourish myself and what products I use that are life-affirming for all of creation, including the animal kingdom.

Chapter Three

Access the Healing Power of Kindness

"The wound is the place where the light enters you."

— RUMI

I remember the cool, crisp March day when cruelty was delivered to me. Someone I held dear in my heart walked, or should I say ran, out of my life in a way that was inhumane, to say the least. It felt like I was beat up and then, while I was down, kicked in the stomach for good measure. The pain and suffering of loss was too much for my heart to bear. My whole world was shaken as the bottom suddenly dropped out.

I was left without recourse in the situation. There was no way to talk to my former friend because the person deleted any attempt I made at contact. There was no way to go back and make it all better because there simply was no communication. It felt like someone took a hammer to my heart and shattered it into a million pieces. I was bleeding from the inside out from this massacre on my heart and could not stop the hurting. The pain was unbearable; and while I was still living, I no longer felt alive. I was left raw with my bleeding wound and wanting so much for it to heal. I clearly remember falling to my knees, sobbing, forgetting everything I knew about positive prayer[1] and crying out to God, "Please, help me."

During this time, a friend of mine said, "You have been betrayed." No, I thought, this was not betrayal because the person who suddenly abandoned me didn't owe me friendship. Everyone gets to make their own choices and that includes the choice to run away. Upon examining the issue of betrayal more closely, I found that it was right on target. Betrayal is one of the most debilitating of all the wounds you can face. You see, betrayal isn't just about cheating on someone, acting dishonestly and hiding addictions or financial transactions. It is about any promise, overt or implied, that has been broken without your participation in the decision, or even knowing that a decision was being made. This is precisely why the first reaction to betrayal is denial. We are shocked and can't believe it's true. We feel disoriented and stunned. It is earth-shattering to discover that what we thought was our reality was not.

As Jean Houston writes in her book, *The Search for the Beloved,* "Betrayal of all the woundings that may be suffered by the soul can be the greatest agent of the sacred.

This wound has always had an awful and luminous quality surrounding it. It marks the end of primal, unconscious trust, and forces upon us those terrible conditions that accompany the taking of the next step.... The condition of this trust has been a subtle and powerful binding that blocks the fullness of the greater consciousness needed to respond to new situations—situations that cannot be met within the old conditions."

Betrayal is different from other wounds. You have been blindsided, and your trust in the human race is gone. You can't trust your own perceptions, nor can you trust other people. It is the end of an age of innocence so to speak. Worse yet, many blame themselves for the betrayal and heap guilt on top of anger, sorrow, and disorientation. We certainly feel naïve and stupid that we didn't see it coming and that our innocence is abolished. You can hide behind extravagant shopping sprees, alcoholism, promiscuity, gambling, or becoming a workaholic, but there is no running away from the pain and no seeming upside to betrayal or the effects it has on one's life. If we numb the pain with external resources, we never fully engage in living or in healing.

Yet no matter how much we resist the effects of betrayal, the only way out of the pain is to move toward it and to allow the sacred to take over. Don't avoid the pain because this is an opportunity for deep transformation. Instead, gather the gifts the pain brings and learn and grow from it. Don't deny that the experience happened by attempting to reframe it (because it did happen the way you perceived it to happen—in other words, validate your feelings to yourself); rather, flow with it instead of swimming against the stream. While it may not seem like it at the time, powerful growth is taking place beneath the surface, and you will heal, because in reality you were never broken to begin with.

Embrace the beauty of a newly transformed you that has been birthed out of the sorrow.

A Sacred Space

Yes, trust has been shaken to the core after a betrayal, and sadness tunnels through your entire being. Yet the experience creates space for growth and expansion of heart. If we could love in spite of the gaping wound of betrayal, if we could open our hearts with compassion, if we could dig deep and find that the light of the Divine is ever present within us and cannot be extinguished no matter how someone behaves toward us, we have a space for the sacred and wise. Betrayal is cruel. It can make us bitter or it can remind us to grow closer to our Source. Our experience in the aftermath can generate gratitude for everything good in our lives, including the wound. In our wounded state, we have an unparalleled opportunity to give ourselves completely over to God. We can allow ourselves to be recreated into something new and better.

Loss may be the most transformative event that can happen to us. Although loss leaves a hole in our hearts, this is the space where God rushes in to fill the vacuum with love and light. Certainly it does not feel like it while we are in the midst of severe grief, but something greater is waiting for us after we move through the pain. If anyone would have told me that I would later be grateful for the experience of betrayal for giving me an expanded opportunity to practice kindness, love, and forgiveness while I could strengthen my connection with God, I would have shrugged it off as nonsense. Yet it is true.

Compassion blossoms after the experience of suffering and loss, and cruelty is often the gateway to kindness. From our loss, pain, and heartache comes a feeling of loving ourselves and others. The most potent remedy for heartache is to give love and kindness to others. When your heart hurts, give love and watch something miraculous happen. For me, amid the pain, confusion and turmoil, I accepted a sacred invitation to lay aside my ego and extend deep compassion and kindness to myself and others. What I thought was an eternal wound transformed into a light that guided me to serving others in a most humble and uplifting way.

Authentic kindness sprouts from the bleeding heart. Love grows more beautifully after the most painful blows to the heart. We become fortified and strengthened, and our wholeness is revealed after the devastation of suffering. We discover courage and wisdom in the face of suffering. Kindness brings us back to our true compassionate nature.

Spiritual Bypasses

Most of us have faced tragic situations in our lifetimes, whether from betrayal, heartbreak, loss, abuse or some other circumstance. Maybe you lost your job, lost a loved one, received a diagnosis of a serious health condition or suffered physical violence at the hands of someone else. In such tragic times, many well-meaning spiritual people will try to lay platitudes on you.

These invalidating spiritual platitudes, which are often referred to as spiritual bypasses, don't help and can actually worsen someone's pain. Sayings like "It's all good," "You created this," "It is God's will," "It is all in divine order," are not helpful or constructive. When someone is going through emotional devastation feeling like a stake has pierced the heart, it does not feel like "it" is all good. If suffering loss of a loved one, saying it is God's will doesn't change the fact that a heart aches for one who has passed on.

Spiritual seekers often want to escape from feeling pain and cover it up with these trite little sayings. These people imply you are negative if you speak about your grief. From experience facilitating bereavement groups for hospice patients and for suicide survivors, I can tell you that talking about your pain is not negativity, nor is it a sign of spiritual weakness. Talking with others who understand and validate you is one of the most healing steps on the journey of grief. Holding your feelings in and donning the mask of a happy face is more damaging to you than letting your feelings out. In times of loss, it is extremely important to grieve; and talking to friends, relatives, professionals or people in a support group helps as long as they are supportive and know how to listen.

It is not beneficial to talk to people who advise you to get over your grief by, for example, going to the movies, getting a facial, taking a pill, scheduling a massage, or starting a juice diet. These suggestions oversimplify the situation and invalidate what someone is feeling. Well-meaning but unaware people may also lay blame on you for expressing your pain, even possibly suggesting (or saying outright) that you are perpetuating the pain for a self-serving or attention-seeking purpose. What is important to remember is that suffering does not mean we should shoulder blame ourselves for our pain. Neither is suffering something to be embarrassed by or to be compared with others' reactions to life events. Some will say, "It's too bad you are perpetuating this pain you say you feel. You should have had positive thoughts. You should have practiced coping strategies better." To say this is to deny your (and their) uniqueness as a thinking, feeling individual in the situation; your perspectives will never be the same.

We don't want to take the blame for what has happened; however, we can take responsibility for contributing to the situation that caused our pain, if appropriate. Ultimately, though, when people betray you, lie, or misrepresent themselves, it is their choice to do so. Betrayal indicates their emotional and spiritual immaturity, not yours. In betraying you, others are demonstrating that they are not of a consciousness that can honor your feelings or reveal who they really are. In kindness, then, we pray that their consciousness may be raised so they can become aware and grow.

No matter what the situation, we don't need to make someone feel spiritually inferior or heap guilt onto someone's shoulders when the heart is suffering or grieving. There is no blame required to dole out for difficult times. True spiritual wisdom comes from knowing what is important and what will you do going forward. Dr. Ernest Holmes, founder of Religious Science, taught us that what thought has done, thought can undo. This concept was never meant to blame someone for their experience, but inspire people to not only think from the highest state of consciousness but deliberately sow seeds of goodness in their thoughts to create a better-acted future. Sowing seeds of kindness is needed now precisely because tomorrow is the result of today's thoughts and actions. You have a choice between wallowing in blame, shame, and guilt or being courageous and becoming stronger from the pain. Look for the kindness and grace that is around you.

The result of spiritual bypasses, then, is a combination of invalidation and blame, and that is never healing. Healing comes from what we do with the suffering we have faced. Do we grow? Do we learn? Do we become kinder and more connected to God? Certainly we gain valuable wisdom from the experience. This wisdom, coupled with loving ourselves and treating ourselves gently, will generate healing. Suffering hurts. That's the hard and fast truth. However, the secret to healing is not letting time pass but by letting kindness pass from you to others. Pure unconditional love for ourselves and others will take the wounded heart to a sacred healing ground where the Divine lives within you.

The fact is that we are human and in our lifetimes we will face loneliness, sorrow, betrayal, and tragic circumstances. Instead of numbing our pain with external measures such as prescription drugs, alcohol, shopping and pornography, we must lean in to move through it with grace and growth. If we don't let ourselves feel the pain, we miss the opportunity to spread our wings and welcome renewal into our lives. We miss the potential for the joy that comes when we have deepened our connection with the ever-loving Divine Presence within. It does hurt like crazy to experience cruelty. But when we become aware of the fact that running from pain doesn't help, we can use these experiences to transform expressions of dismay into inspiration. Our woundedness is an opportunity for greater giving and is often the impetuous toward walking the path to awakening. These transforming moments in which we suffer today will soon be known when the Divine birthed a new version of ourselves. For the difficulties we face are teaching opportunities, and by feeling and transcending them, we accelerate our spiritual growth. Struggles therefore can help us learn compassion, kindness, and understanding.

This point is illustrated in Logion 58 from the *Gospel of Thomas* when Jesus says, "Blessed are those who have undergone ordeals. They have entered into life." This means that those of us who walk a sacred path use our wounds as tools for teachings that propel us toward enlightenment. Life is to be lived and learned through every situation; avoidance or denial of the trials and tribulations keeps us stagnant and in lower states of awareness. It is not only possible, but necessary, to grow through suffering and come away with deeper understanding of our spiritual selves.

Covering up our agony with spiritual platitudes is hollow, useless, and almost as bad as turning to drinking, drugs, gambling or other addictions to run from pain. Instead of running from the hurt, move toward it, feel it, and let it wash over you. There's nothing amiss by feeling the pain. We are not spiritually damaged—suffering is part of the human condition. We are not less spiritual if we feel pain. It's what we do with suffering that makes us spiritual. More suffering takes place when we protect ourselves from feeling our pain. Often repressed feelings manifest as illness down the road. This is why we need to be with the pain, facing it head on and trusting that it will pass as the clouds pass by the Sun on a cloudy day. Just like our inner light is always present, the shining rays of the Sun are always there, only temporarily covered by the clouds passing by.

Remember that when our hearts break, it's an opening for more love, more compassion, more communication with God. When things get impossibly painful, there is only one thing that will heal. That is the healing power of kindness. One drop of kindness can mend a shattered heart even if it's just one piece at a time.

Think of the great spiritual teachers and mystics that experienced suffering and betrayal such as Jesus, Buddha, St. Francis of Assisi, and St. John of the Cross. There's an ancient story about Buddha that takes place on the eve of his enlightenment. The Buddha, who was known as a bodhisattva (someone who has taken a special vow committing himself to compassionately serving others), sat under the Bodhi Tree, determined to stay there until he was enlightened. Mara, a mythical figure in the Buddhist tradition known as the "killer of virtue" and the "killer of life," recognized that his kingdom of delusion was put at risk by the bodhisattva's longing to awaken and thus developed several perilous challenges for him. Mara longed to get the bodhisattva to give up his quest for enlightenment, so he challenged him through lust, anger, and fear. Mara plagued the bodhisattva with hailstorms, mud storms, and other problems. No matter what occurred, the bodhisattva sat peacefully, unwavering in his resolution. The final challenge of Mara was self-doubt. He said to the bodhisattva, "By what right are you even sitting there with that goal? What makes you think you have the right even to aspire to full enlightenment, to complete awakening?" Unmoved by Mara's taunts, the bodhisattva reached over and touched the Earth. He called upon the Earth itself to bear witness to all of the lifetimes that he had practiced generosity, patience, and morality. Throughout his many lifetimes, he had built a wave of moral empowerment that had given him the right of aspiration and resistance to all taunts.

Kindness Heals

When we are plagued with hail storms in our lives—the painful situations that literally sink us to our knees—we can take comfort by knowing that kindness heals. It is not just kindness that others show us that heals, it is also kindness that we give to others. During my time of suffering from the loss of a dear friend, healing came to me from the process of practicing kindness to others. In my work, I have many opportunities to do this. Just being present with a dying person or a suicide survivor and praying for the person renews my soul, and I can feel my heart cracking open wide and love pouring out from me. This lovingkindness heals all wounds and takes us through the pain to the other side, which is joy.

Grief's Silver Lining

The struggles you face today are opportunities for new ways of being to grow. Grief, as heart-shattering as it is, opens up the avenues of expressing greater love. Through grief we can cultivate more understanding, patience, compassion, and empathy. It's not like we want grief to come into our lives, but it is inevitable that at some point we will experience the sting of grief that accompanies loss. Amid the suffering, there is an opening for deep transformation. My experience, for example, opened my heart and was instrumental in transforming me to a gentler, kinder, more loving person—qualities that may have not developed so deeply had I not experienced suffering. It also moved me to delve more deeply into spiritual studies and to become a more empathic spiritual coach and chaplain. I found awakening from this time of pain ignited the transformative spark of kindness deep within my soul. Experiences of cruelty also led me to write about kindness and foster a deep longing in my heart to alleviate the suffering of others. While I wouldn't say that suffering is required to do heartfelt work, it can be an agent of change within us and propel us into the yearning to help others in their times of distress.

Some claim that painful situations are karmic (karma is the law of cause and effect, or you might think of it as, "As you sow, so shall you reap") and that the person who hurt you simply delivered your karma to you. By this construct, he or she is the messenger. Taking the stance that it's your karma and you are at fault, that the hurt you inflicted has boomeranged back upon you, places needless blame on yourself, adding blame to the sense of loss. People who look at life events this way question themselves at every turn, wondering, *What did I do to cause this?* And, *Am I a bad person to have attracted this situation?* Blaming yourself for bad experiences is disempowering and does not do any good. Karma blame is not the same as being accountable for your actions; it is destructive and painful. I have heard it said somewhere that karma is not a punishment, but a correction. I certainly like that point of view and would much prefer to be corrected than punished, although ultimately I would rather invite us to look for the opportunities for personal growth.

In the *Heart Sutra,* the Dalai Lama says, "Karma refers to actions undertaken with intention. And given that the entire development of our unenlightened existence is a consequence of our undisciplined state of mind, in the final analysis, the mind is the creator of our entire existence. Karma is what fuels the whole evolution of an individual's existence in samsara." According to the Dalai Lama, samsara is an "endless cycle of suffering, of enduring countless rounds of birth and death." A Buddhist teacher once explained to me that when causes and conditions are right, the karma plays out. While it may be a stretch for some people to believe, I read somewhere that we should be grateful to those who hurt us because these situations open the door for us to work off karma in this lifetime. When we have exhausted our karma, we attain enlightenment.

By contrast, some people believe we agreed to these experiences on the other side before we were born because we made a soul contract then that is simply being carried out during this lifetime. Perhaps we made a contract with someone that we would endure this trauma and learn greater love, compassion, patience, forgiveness or some other virtue. Don't get too caught up in analyzing whether or not your situation is the result of karma or a soul contract because no matter what the cause, you are experiencing events at the present moment. We can't change what happened in the past, but we can choose the seeds that we plant for future experiences. Planting seeds of kindness lifts us up even in our hour of despair.

The healing power of kindness is vast and wide. Regarding all our life's experiences, including ones of suffering, as part of our sacred journey inspires us to take a leap of faith and trust that life is a work in progress. With a broader perspective, we can look at what's happening with the gentle eyes of kindness and feel propelled forward to a life filled with joy. Look at the difficult situations in your life and allow them to awaken the kind heart that lives within you. This is the silver lining tucked away in your grief and the way to transform suffering into joy and pain into peace.

Kindness in Action

As a single mom and a hardworking woman, Pamela Sills felt she could pull herself up by her bootstraps and overcome challenges, no matter what occurred. However, she was unprepared for the storm that was about to erupt in her life when her second husband's personality began to change, resulting in violent outbursts of both physical and emotional abuse. Pam says, "One of his explosions was the final one. He was briefly hospitalized after raging and becoming suicidal." Despite this, Pam held out hope for the marriage and they went to counseling while her husband stayed at a neutral place. Suddenly the bottom dropped out. Pam's husband disappeared to another state to live with a former romantic partner, taking all of their financial assets with him, even the commissions that he and Pam had earned together while working at a major radio communications company. Pam was left penniless and abandoned with creditors breathing down her neck.

Pam vividly recalls sitting in the living room and literally going into shock. "I was paralyzed," she said, "I had no idea what to do. There were no assets and I couldn't afford the place where we were living." She stayed with her son and his wife at first and then moved in with her elderly parents. Her parents' home offered no refuge, though; her father was suffering from Alzheimer's and, due to his disease and unresolved emotional issues, he targeted his daughter for his frequent angry outbursts.

Pam left her parents' home but could not get a lease on her own place even though she was working again. She briefly house-sat for a friend and mentally prepared to live out of her car if necessary. Just before that would become the new low point in her life, a friend put her in touch with Russell, a ninety-year-old man who offered to rent Pam the whole bottom half of his home. This was the first act of kindness that saved and restored her; in fact, Pam called Russell her "first angel." The time at Russell's home was healing for both of them. Evenings, this frail elderly gentleman and traumatized woman sat on the couch companionably holding hands and laughing at television sitcoms. Pam said she felt "safe and protected there." The stay was cut short, unfortunately, when Russell's family asked her to vacate even though it broke the man's heart to see her go.

Once again the search for an apartment began while depression tunneled through the core of her being. At her lowest point, Pam noticed Neighbor's Place—A Residence for Women, a beautiful apartment building that was subsidized by donations and charity work. Pam called and left a message indicating she'd been homeless for one year and didn't think she could keep going without a place to live. After leaving this voicemail, Pam drove to the office to see if she could plead her case in person. Amazingly, the manager said, "We have a place for you right now." This second act of extraordinary kindness set Pam on a path of healing.

Just as Pam was signing the lease at Neighbor's Place, the owner Paul Schreiner walked in. He told her he was the executive director of Project Neighbors, a nonprofit agency with the goal of building healthy families and neighborhoods welcoming diversity of all kinds. He said it was his idea to establish new resources for the downtrodden and draw from the community for support. Pam could avail herself of all their help including life skills education, social events, food pantry items, furniture and basic necessities, all in a safe and comfortable environment. Pam broke down when she met Paul. She told him, "I can't express how much this means to me. Not only that you are giving me a place to lease but you are restoring my dignity and my life." She described it as a "kindness beyond anything she imagined would come her way."

"During that dark time in my life, I felt like my life was over," Pam said, "with nothing in my future: nothing going forward and nothing ever happening in my life again. What they restored to me was my life. If not for those angels and those acts of kindness and compassion, I may not be alive today."

For one solid year Pam was in a living nightmare that she couldn't wake up from. But glimmers of kindness changed her world. She forgave her ex-husband and has a successful career in holistic health. Pam recounted, "If it hadn't been for Neighbor's Place, I would not have been able to take those steps." She said, "Every seeming negative circumstance, sometimes even the worst of circumstances, brings us our greatest gifts. As hard as it may be at the moment to believe there's anything beyond for you in your life, know that as dark as it gets, there is hope that your life can come back bigger and better for you in ways you cannot see and feel at that time. Just know that it can and will happen."

Affirmation

No matter what is going on in the world of form, I have an eternal source of courage, love, and peace flowing through me, guiding me to a brighter day.

Chapter Four

Be a Little Kind to Your Self

"We are in the habit of identifying ourselves with our bodies. The idea that we are this body is deeply entrenched in us. But we are not just this body; we are much more than that. The idea that 'This body is me and I am this body' is an idea we must get rid of. If we do not we will suffer a great deal. We are life, and life is far vaster than this body."

— THICH NHAT HANH

The external world is constantly sending us messages that we are not good enough or there is something wrong with us. Just think of the beauty industry alone. Everywhere you look, whether it's on television, in magazines or on social media, messages say that we have to do something about our crepey skin, sagging jawlines, weight, bust line, crow's feet, you name it; we are left with the impression that one way or another, we don't likely measure up to the fabricated ideal. In our youth-obsessed culture, aging is portrayed as an enemy to be avoided at all costs rather than a life stage to be revered and cherished. Watch any sitcom on television and you will hear insensitive jokes about elderly people. Many messages shout at us that we have to reach a certain economic status, drive a certain car, or go on lavish vacations to be happy; if we fall short of the projected ideals, we are apt to feel dejected and inferior. Perhaps people you looked up to as a child labeled you as stupid, sloppy, untalented or unattractive. Sadly, these messages are taken in by the subconscious mind and become ingrained in our consciousness; as a result, we accept them as truth. It's no wonder that, as a result of this barrage of misguided messages, our society suffers an epidemic of suicides, eating disorders, low self-esteem, cutting on the physical body, regret, guilt, shame, resentments, judgment, and critical self-talk.

Many of our beliefs about ourselves are simply not true. We identify with what we look like, what we do, what we earn, and what talents we have, but these external factors are not who we are. They don't define us and never will. Our society will convince you that if you buy this certain product, reach a certain level of wealth, or participate in the latest fad, you will become complete. In fact, marketing campaigns are designed to make you feel badly about yourself and broken so that you will buy products and procedures they tell you will make you happy. The truth is you are complete right now, right where you are. You are a unique child of God, and God did not make a mistake in creating you. If we focus our thoughts on seeming shortcomings, that is precisely what will manifest in our world because what we think becomes our experience.

It's time to shift away from the mass consciousness and making dangerous comparisons to others. It's time to give tender-hearted compassion to ourselves. You may never fit into those size-two jeans or achieve that gap between your thighs unless you starve yourself, but so what? Do those false attributes define you as a person? Not at all. It is urgent that we stop the comparisons to others. Loving and caring for ourselves means recognizing that the Divine is expressed by us.

Start practicing lovingkindness to yourself in order to genuinely extend it to others. We must slam the door on any thoughts that say we are unworthy or unlovable. We must stop the conversation in our heads that is critical and judgmental of ourselves. We can look at past mistakes without guilt and shame, but as wonderful opportunities for awakening and transformation.

Many coaching clients come to me with low self-esteem and berate themselves in their speech. If this is a barometer of how you live, understand that this toxic conversation in your mind is a deep-rooted pattern, a tape that you have played for a lifetime that sabotages the ability for peace, love, and joy. When we are immersed in judgment and criticism, we have no room to enjoy the bliss of living. All too often we are unaware of destructive thought patterns and first must see them to deplete their power. Once you are aware of these false thoughts, you can shift this behavior. The first step is to treat yourself how you would a friend; you would never speak so harshly to a beloved friend as you might to yourself. I encourage you to cultivate tenderness toward yourself and to see the truth behind the mask: you are good enough. If you hear a voice telling you that you are damaged goods or broken in some way, it is a lie.

Barbara Gulbranson

Busting Cultural Myths

I have not always been self-actualized or self-loving. In fact, my journey on this path has been long. Like many of us, I took my early cues about beauty and desirability from the media. When I was a teenager, I read *Seventeen* magazine with my friends and formed my opinion of beauty from supermodels like Twiggy, Cheryl Tiegs, and Christy Brinkley. In addition, a mean-spirited comment about my figure from a boy I liked only solidified my body image issues. My subconscious mind took the message of "not as good as others" as truth well into adulthood no matter how many positive messages followed.

In my forties, the wife/mother of my favorite sitcom was proportioned much like a Barbie doll which frankly looks fake and, as we know, is unrealistic. This actress has admitted to multiple cosmetic surgeries; yet even though intellectually I knew better, looking at her still convinced me that was the ideal. It didn't matter that I was a grown woman with a sound mind; this cultural influence of unrealistic beauty standards can influence anyone at any age.

My self-esteem was low and I was critical of my appearance, so the show's effect on me was magnified. The fact that my body had changed made it worse: like many women, after having a C-section my stomach muscles had separated, creating a bulge that looked like I was five months pregnant. In fact, my midsection was several sizes larger than the rest of my petite body, and finding clothes to fit was a heart-shattering ordeal. I was in great shape, worked out at the gym several times a week, and ate healthfully, but no amount of exercise or good eating habits could correct the misshapen area.

I remember the day when I took my daughter swimming at a local pool and felt deeply ashamed of my midsection, trying to hide it as I indulged in dangerous mental comparisons to the other moms. Believing that I was ugly and deformed, especially in comparison to the sitcom's wife/mother ideal, I had a tummy tuck plastic surgery. This is a serious surgery and recovery is not to be taken lightly. Sadly, the surgery did not work. The physician did not repair the muscles and I was left looking worse than I had been before. I still had the bulge, but now I was asymmetrical–one side of my waist curved in but the other did not. The doctor refused to make a correction and denied what had happened. When I attained mediation for a refund or a correction, the doctor defamed my character. I was left depleted, hurt, and emotionally scarred from the experience. Over and over I asked, "Why me? Why did my surgery get botched?"

The surgical experience ultimately facilitated deep transformation within my soul. I see now that the debilitating experience of failed cosmetic surgery was something that had to happen before I could change and grow. Over the time of healing, I came to a place where I had to let go of the anger and victimization I felt in order to live a happy life. I had to surrender to Spirit and trust that this experience was something I personally had to go through for my growth. Years later, I found another surgeon who was able to correct the separated muscles, but could not correct the asymmetry. This second surgery was the final turning point. I had to release any and all attachment to my physical form. I would never look like the actress on television. I had to let it go. This was my personal lesson to learn: I had to release attachment to the physical form and really understand in my mind and heart that every happening is a blessing for my greater good. I moved from a place of despair to gratitude and could then receive joy. This was a gift from Spirit, to learn to love myself as I am and to shed attachment to the physical form. Shedding attachment to form is vital to happiness. The Buddhists, in fact, teach that attachment to form is the cause of all suffering.

Experiencing this torment in my own life would be a catalyst to greater growth and compassion in helping other women who have similar feelings about their looks and low self-esteem. Coming from a place of having been there, I can deeply feel the struggle people have with their weight, appearance, wrinkles, economic status, or whatever is their own bane. A result of feeling this pain prompted me to want to take everyone who has these issues by the hand and whisper, "You are good enough. You are strong, powerful, and beautiful just as you are. Your magnificent energy radiates out from you and lights up the world."

From Powerless to Empowerment

My own journey from low self-esteem to empowerment gives me the understanding to encourage you to release any feelings of inferiority and recognize that all the beauty of God is revealed through you. Your beauty is always present and radiating out toward others. Your beauty is not the same as someone else's, nor would you want it to be. Celebrate your uniqueness and abolish the unkind comparisons to others that will weigh you down like a ton of bricks. Right now, feel the radiant energy of your beauty and be confident that the Divine light within you shines brighter than anything you do on the outer realm. Turn away from the cultural myths and that old recording playing in your head, and connect with the wellspring of beauty within you. Turn off the infomercial that says you need this or that product to be of value. You are all the beauty, grace, and elegance of the God within you. No surgical procedure, no cosmetic product, no antiaging formulation can outdo the magnificent work of the Spirit manifesting as you. Trust that your beauty truly is within and let the former you slip away. Celebrate the emergence of the true beautiful you. Embrace all that you are including your physical form which is the precious vehicle through which Spirit expresses as you.

Please keep in mind that I am not saying cosmetic surgery is to be avoided. That is a personal decision each person has to make for him or herself. It could be a positive decision with great results if done with a healthy attitude and an understanding that happiness is truly an inside job; nothing on the outside can manufacture happiness. My experience illustrates the growth I personally needed to go through in this lifetime, which took place in this particular way. Your experience will not be the same as mine as we all walk our sacred journey in our own way.

If you have any feelings of unworthiness, say:

> *I am more than my body. I am created in the image*
> *and likeness of God. I love and embrace all of me.*
> *I am an empowered and magnificent creation of*
> *Spirit in whom all beauty resides.*

Practicing Self-Kindness

Consider embracing who you really are. All too often we forget that we are extensions of Spirit having a human experience through us. Knowing this, how then could you be cruel toward yourself? Ways to cultivate kindness for yourself include:

- Practicing self-care each day by eating healthfully, meditating, walking in nature, praying, listening to soothing music, or whatever nourishes your mind, body, and spirit.
- Thinking back to the good you have done in your life. Have you given love to a child, rescued an abused animal, helped someone in need or acted out of compassion toward others?
- Reflecting back to a mistake you made and thinking about how you have grown and risen in consciousness from the experience. Remember, there are no mistakes, only opportunities for greater growth and expansion of heart.
- Becoming your own best friend and treating yourself with love and kindness. When judgment or criticism arises, ask,

"Is this how I would speak about a friend?" The Divine is your eternal friend and enfolds you in love and light. It's time to take your rightful place as a child of God and accept the gift, the grace, and the glory of knowing you are worthy of unconditional love.

- Extending kindness not only to the parts of yourself that you deem "good" but to all of the facets of yourself, even those you label "imperfect."
- Using affirmations (positive statements of truth) when feelings of unworthiness arise such as, *I am a worthy child of God. I give and receive love fully. My compassionate nature is expanded. My beauty radiates out to all of life. I am of value and fulfill my life's purpose on Earth.* Transforming negative thoughts into positive ones rewires your subconscious mind and changes unwanted patterns of negative self-talk. That's because the subconscious mind takes your new positive thoughts and transforms them into a new and greater reality.
- Avoiding the comparison trap. Don't compare yourself to others because that is a toxic practice. Instead, celebrate your uniqueness and revel in what you have to offer the world.
- Making a commitment to being kind to yourself. Write down a statement of your intention to practice lovingkindness toward yourself and sign and date it. Making this promise to yourself is a major step in changing unwanted patterns and making space for joy, comfort, and peace.

Taking these measures will shift the energy from self-loathing to self-love and give rise to lovingkindness toward yourself. What a relief to know that you can release beliefs that are not true about you and never were true. When we eliminate our feelings of unworthiness, our true nature is revealed and life unfolds in a harmonious way. Be sure to be persistent in uprooting the negative thoughts that seep into your consciousness and remember that who you are is much greater than your looks or economic status. Trust that Spirit knows how to work through you and there is an abundance of good awaiting upon your acceptance of this truth.

Be gentle and kind with yourself and watch how your life changes in miraculous ways. This practice of kindness toward yourself will lay the groundwork for authentic kindness toward others to grow. Trust in the universe. Let go of all those lies that say, "I'm not good enough." Truth is you are good enough—you are more than good enough. You are worthy of every blessing and gift that the universe has for you. Let the seed of compassion take root in your consciousness and allow it to grow into full fruition. Let kindness for yourself expand and as a result it will expand out to others. This is how you will change your life and change your encounters with others.

Kindness in Action

Julia, a stunning and intelligent twenty-two-year-old woman, has struggled with an eating disorder since her early teens. As an overweight child and preteen, she developed low self-esteem and a body image disorder. Stopping eating and committing self-harm were ways to punish herself and cope with her perceived imperfections.

Julia tells us, "My eating disorder led me to not only harming myself by cutting but also by going to the gym two hours a day and walking vigorously on the treadmill for hours at a time." Learning to be kind to herself given the harshness of what she was doing to her body was a daunting task for Julia.

The turning point was when her boyfriend gave her an ultimatum: "Get professional help or I will leave you." This was an eye-opener and motivated her to see a therapist who practiced dialectical behavioral therapy (DBT). One of the best things that Julia learned with DBT was mindfulness, which taught her to be aware of the present moment and to just 'be' without trying to change the moment."

Another turning point for Julia was getting a comfort animal which allows her to give and receive unconditional love freely. She tells us that having that connection with her rescue dog is fulfilling and rewarding, "Your pet's love for you is unconditional and to have that in your life helps calm anxiety and calm the bad thoughts. If you feel you hate yourself, getting an emotional support pet will help you feel better."

Julia admits that the media has had an enormous effect on her body image. Recently on social media photos have appeared of celebrities that were not altered by Photoshop, and one famous person with a beautiful body actually has cellulite illustrating that everyone's body is not perfect.

Another way Julia learned to be kind to herself was by adopting a vegetarian diet. This helped give her control over her diet and allowed her to get more calories and eat in a healthful manner.

One of the greatest kindnesses on this journey of healing is from her therapist who shows her compassion and understanding. Julia said, "I can text or call my therapist any time I experience a panic attack and she will answer."

While Julia says that once you have an eating disorder it never goes entirely away, she has learned to overcome the harshness of this eating disorder. Learning to love your body is a process. "The best thing I could recommend is to learn to love your flaws and accept yourself. You are your body your whole life. Make it your home and don't treat it like a dump. Treat your body like it's the best thing there is. You're wasting time and energy staring at everything that is wrong with it."

Please note: *Nine out of ten deaths of people suffering from anorexia nervosa are from suicide. Because anorexics develop a fearlessness of harming themselves, and often have co-occurring conditions such as depression, anxiety or substance abuse, it puts them at a great risk of suicide. If someone you know has an eating disorder, take them for professional help immediately.*

Affirmation

I am gentle and kind to myself just like I would be to a dear friend. I release any and all thoughts of unworthiness and stand up tall as a beautiful, empowered creation of God for whom all things are possible.

Chapter Five

Get Your Attitude On

"All the joy the world contains has come through wishing happiness for others. All the misery the world contains has come through wanting pleasure for oneself."
— SHANTIDEVA

Opening the pathways to joy takes attitude—a bodhichitta attitude, that is. With what Buddhists call bodhichitta attitude, we find a source of happiness beyond what we have ever imagined before. Bodhichitta attitude is for everyone, no matter what your faith tradition. It's a mindset that aligns you with the Divine Presence within, which is always there just waiting for you to access it. This attitude springs from a place within your heart that is tender, open, and completely loving. This attitude is the ultimate in generosity and selflessness to others.

Bodhichitta is a Sanskrit word. "Bodhi" means "awake," and "chitta" means "mind" and "heart." This translates to mean "the awakened heart-mind." Simply put, bodhichitta is the heartfelt need to alleviate suffering in others and help them awaken. Bodhichitta is not just a concern for people, it's a concern for all living creatures as sentient beings who can feel.

Buddhist teacher Sogyal Rinpoche explained it this way: bodhichitta is the "compassionate wish to attain enlightenment for the benefit of all ... it is the spring and source and root of the entire spiritual path. To awaken and develop the heart of the enlightened mind is to ripen steadily the seed of our Buddha nature, that seed that, in the end, when our practice of compassion has become perfect and all-embracing, will flower majestically into Buddhahood."

Bodhichitta is always within us like a flame of love that is never extinguished. It's in growing this authentic garden of kindness in our hearts that we make ourselves receptive to divine gifts and blessings that go beyond Earthly pleasures to deep abiding peace and joy. What, exactly, are you awakening from? You are awakening from those habits, fears, and neuroses that wreak havoc on your emotional well-being. Once you awaken, then you are ready to be instrumental in awakening others on Earth. Having a bodhichitta attitude inspires us to awaken so we can serve others and have an open and brave heart no matter what turmoil is going on around us. Not only is bodhichitta the intense desire to awaken and be free, it is also the aspiration to be liberated from problems not only for ourselves but for others. You can see how this goes beyond random acts of kindness to an intense longing to benefit others and alleviate their suffering.

Why is this attitude important? It opens our hearts and minds toward others whether we are at home, at work, at play or out in the community. It's a good idea each morning upon waking to set your intention on selfless service to others. This, in turn, sets the law of attraction in motion that brings into experience the expressed intention. When you set this intention, you are offering all you have and all you are to other beings. Bodhichitta attitude begins with these brief but powerful words: *May I be God's instrument today.* So when you are having a hard day and your boss is on your case, or you are stuck in traffic and your temper starts to flare—whenever the burdens of life become great: *May I be God's instrument today.* This one small statement moves you away from the stress of the daily grind and realigns you as a vehicle for Spirit to do its work through you. This is how you attain joy that is not fleeting but everlasting.

Someone who has the bodhichitta attitude/motivation and practices is called a bodhisattva. A bodhisattva has taken a special vow to attain enlightenment for all beings. He or she has made a sacred commitment to cultivating compassion and wisdom to free all beings from suffering. This is why the bodhisattva path is often called the path of awakened beings. It is putting others first before ourselves. It is a wish to be an instrument of Spirit to bring about happiness in everyone we meet. It's important to note that this gentleness and kindness is a natural arising, and not a grasping, for happiness. In fact, Buddhist teachings say that grasping after happiness is what actually causes suffering to occur. The goal, then, is for happiness to come naturally from a heightened sense of consciousness, without trying to force it or make it happen. Those with bodhichitta attitude are present today and have been present throughout the ages. Interestingly, His Holiness the Dalai Lama considers Mother Theresa, Martin Luther King, Jr., and Jesus bodhisattvas, so bodhisattvas walk among us in the world and may not always be Buddhists.

A Bodhichitta Thing

Kirby L. Whitacre, author of *Buddhism, A Westerner's Compendium*, explains bodhichitta attitude like this: "There are benefits of getting a bodhichitta attitude. Practice it toward yourself first. You have to have the longing for kindness and altruism toward yourself. When you help others, you feel more moral and more connected and more involved with people and society. At the end of the day you feel you have cared and you have done what you could. This has a real health benefit and a real emotional and mental benefit. It's a huge stress release. Start practicing ethics and you become more moral and you feel better about yourself; you have more integrity and your decisions are not made from a selfish viewpoint but from the viewpoint of the other person. When you consider the other person first, it's a bodhichitta thing."

You already have everything you need within you, including bodhichitta attitude. Working with your inner/higher self and the heart and mind leads to a powerful transformation in how you relate to the world and other people. Thankfully, our heart and mind work together, and we don't have to put a lot of effort into anything because what we are seeking is actually seeking us. The feeling and experience of this enables a tenderness in our hearts to grow. Love automatically springs from our hearts and we feel deep love and compassion for other beings. With this in mind, it's no surprise that a bodhisattva's main goal is to work for enlightenment, not for themselves alone but for all beings. All of the leaders and practitioners of the world's religions would agree that the path to kindness and compassion is for everyone, not just Buddhists.

The key to getting this attitude is in the yearning to be an instrument of love and compassion towards others. In the *Bodhicharyavatara,* or *The Way of the Bodhisattva,* the eighth-century Indian teacher Shantideva says, "Please use me. I prefer to be a bridge, a ship, a highway, a swimming pool, a chariot. Please use me in service of all sentient beings. I have no hesitation. Whatever my situation may be, I am willing to do good for others."

Feelings associated with this attitude include the release of any feelings of unworthiness. You begin to accept yourself and love yourself the way that you are. We realize we are worthy children of God and the kingdom of heaven lies within each one of us. This attitude also cultivates fearlessness. As Lama Anagorika Govinda puts it, "Fearlessness is the most prominent characteristic of all bodhisattvas and all who tread the bodhisattva path. For them, life has lost its terrors and suffering its sting. Instead of scorning earthly existence, or condemning its imperfection, they fill it with new meaning." In the New Thought tradition, we know that fear is feeling separate from God and that we can never be separated from our Source. Love and fear cannot coexist. That's because when one's heart bursts with love, fear cannot be present. When we experience our connectedness with God, it's impossible to be afraid.

Having a bodhichitta attitude is characterized by enjoying life. We have a good sense of humor and relish living life fully. We have an attitude of merriment and partake in life's simple pleasures with joy. With this attitude, we don't shy away from obstacles because they foster growth, heart expansion, and a growing capacity to love. With love, tenderness, gentleness, softness, relaxation, openness, and appreciation at the helm, the bodhisattva enjoys an abiding joy, deep peace, and great satisfaction. Another quality of this attitude is the ability to embrace all feelings. Whether crying, laughing or playing, you feel all your feelings and simply be with them without judging good or bad, wanted or unwanted, right or wrong. With compassion at the forefront of the mind, someone with bodhichitta attitude can connect with all aspects of the true self and experience whatever emotion comes up, fully and freely. In fact, great compassion is unleashed in this beautiful journey of awakening.

People of all time have shared the desire to awaken to their true nature and walk this path. When we develop a gentle heart, well-being and goodness, we can see the same in others, no matter where someone else is in consciousness. It all goes back to the concept of oneness. If we are all interconnected, if we are all one, then we would naturally want to love and serve others. When we see the oneness of all beings, it transforms us and our hearts overflow with love.

Here's how Thubten Yeshe, a Tibetan lama, describes bodhichitta:

> "Bodhichitta is the intoxicant that numbs us against pain and fills us with bliss.
>
> Bodhichitta is the alchemy that transforms every action into benefit for others.
>
> Bodhichitta is the cloud that carries the rain of positive energy to nourish growing things.
>
> Bodhichitta is not doctrine. It is a state of mind. This inner experience is completely individual. So how can we see who is a bodhisattva and who is not? Can we see the self-cherishing mind?
>
> If we feel insecure ourselves, we will project that negative feeling onto others. We need the pure innermost thought of bodhichitta; wherever we go that will take care of us."

A Better World

If, then, you live your life taking the intention of bodhichitta with you, you will experience a deep sense of joy. You will not have any regrets and experience just greater and greater states of happiness. What's more, you will be fully able to help yourself and others on their sacred path. By simply dedicating yourself to assisting others, you will find yourself immersed in bliss consciousness with a calm center of peace at the core of your being. For many people, this leads to a gentleness of character that others gravitate to.

Whitacre tells us that if we all get a bodhichitta attitude, "the world would be the achievement of the ideals of almost every religion. We could focus on medicine, spiritual achievement, the arts, we could get everybody a better lifestyle and concentrate on space. It would be amazing. The land grabbing, the border disputes, the envy; it's all gone. It would eliminate evil, the kidnapping, the murder, the war, and the crooked businesses. It will allow you to spend time on spirituality, conquering disease, and would be like a team effort toward making things even better for humanity."

Indeed, catching the bodhichitta attitude would go a long way toward solving world crises and fostering peace and happiness individually and globally. To deepen bodhichitta attitude, try this practice: go about your day with a quiet gentleness. Whether you are at work, at home or doing errands, carry this tenderness toward everyone you meet. Yes, even toward the grouchy customer you come across, the person who directs road rage at you or anyone who takes out their frustrations on you. Maintain that quality of tenderness no matter how someone behaves toward you. Then take this a step further and practice tenderness with yourself. Move away from blame, guilt, or shame and cease thinking something you said or did was stupid. In each sacred moment of your day, practice tenderness. You can do this as often as you like until it is, even for one hour, etched in your heart as ingrained an activity as brushing your teeth in the morning. If you find yourself moving away from this tenderness and begin berating yourself, gently bring your intention back to that tender heart. You might start feeling bubbles of bliss, which is natural when you are expanding your heart and letting the light of God shine through you.

Tenderness toward yourself and others is the first step in cultivating bodhichitta attitude. It's a critical step that the world is crying out for in all its chaos and pain. We can do this collectively as a society to infuse the Earth with the compassion and love it craves. While the bodhisattva path may not be for everyone, it is for individuals of any faith tradition who want to make a difference in themselves and the world. We can use everything that happens in our life, every difficulty, obstacle and challenge, as fuel for change in consciousness. As Buddhist teacher, Trungpa Rinpoche, said, "Whatever occurs in the confused mind is regarded as the path. Everything is workable. It is a fearless proclamation, the lion's roar."

If every circumstance is on the path, then we walk on sacred ground. We can tread that ground with lovingkindness toward every sentient being and use the experience of suffering to move toward greater understanding and enlightenment. With bodhichitta attitude, we can renew the world by strengthening our capacity for kindness and by finding that tender spot of compassion within, allowing it to grow out from ourselves to touch the hearts of many and lift up those who are suffering.

Kindness in Action

Bodhisattvas who have the heartfelt longing to alleviate suffering in others walk among us in our daily lives. One person who exemplifies this trait is Fe Anam Avis, author of *A Second Day: A Hopeful Journey out of Suicidal Thinking* and founder of Soul Shop™, an organization with the mission of fostering transformation in faith communities by equipping them to minister to those impacted by suicidal desperation. With its vision to equip leaders from 20,000 congregations by 2020, Soul Shop™ trains faith leaders to help those who have never considered suicide to sharpen their compassion and understanding for those who have, people who are considering suicide, people who are concerned about a loved one or friend who may be considering suicide, and those who know someone who died from suicide. The organization also focuses on Second Day people—those who were suicidal in the past but are no longer. This organization differs from others because it not only focuses on those who attempted suicide but on those who experience suicidal desperation. It includes people living in the darkness of that thinking and people who have lost someone and feel they can't talk about it due to the shame and stigma of it.

Fe himself is a Second Day person. He says, "I didn't value myself to allow my voice to be heard. I did not pay attention to my own soul and give it adequate voice, which led me to that level of desperation." As a former minister, Fe put the needs of others first and as the oldest child in his family the expectation was that he would be the expression of the family. From a place of desperation, Fe went to buy a gun to kill himself. At some point, however, he changed his mind, which he attributes to Divine intervention. He tells it like this: "I had been at the lowest of low and had to go to my parents' home and stay there for the evening alone to check on their house in the country while they were away. I went there and my family, which is a hunting family, had guns at the house. This was the lowest point in my life."

As Fe was experiencing suicidal thinking, his fiancée Shawn was trying to call him but Fe was isolating himself as he often does when experiencing pain. He lay down on the bed that he had slept in as a boy and the image of a face appeared looking directly into his face. The face was saying, "Breathe; don't you leave me. Breathe." And for that one half hour he would see this face every time he closed his eyes and he'd hear those words. A week later Fe was on a hike with his fiancée, who is now his wife, and he sat down to rest and said, "I need to tell you about this experience I had." As Fe told her what happened, tears streamed down her face and she said, "I was so worried for you when you wouldn't answer the phone. I prayed that God would send an angel to you." The compassion and kindness that Shawn showed by praying was instrumental in saving Fe's life.

Fe believes he was looking into the face of an angel that God had sent, which gave him an experience he could reflect back on and remember that it protected him. He felt love coming from the angel. It was a powerful sense of love that he had trouble mustering for himself. Having a face looking into his face—normally you don't let anyone get that close to you. The intensity of that face in front of his face and this plea, "Don't you leave me," carried with it such a sense that he was important to this being. That sense of importance of his life in a mysterious but universal sense was very powerful, Fe tells us.

He explains that it is not only angels but people who can give us gifts that we cannot give ourselves at times. Eventually we must learn to give to ourselves the kindness and love we need; sometimes it comes from other people and we need to borrow it because we don't have it ourselves. It gives us a connection to people who care about us and it gives us a sense of if one person can care about us maybe others can. Fe says, "You can experience kindness and love from people in an instant that can be powerful. The love of God is channeled through people," Fe explains. In fact, the Christmas message, for example, is that the love of God must be given flesh and blood expression. God so loved the world that he sent a flesh and blood person. There is no substitute for experiencing the love of God through another human being. Fe relates this to a sign he saw in Ft. Hood, TX, that said, "Thinking of suicide? Call on Jesus." He can appreciate that, but the reality is that when we are that desperate we need a flesh and blood person that can give expression to the love of Jesus.

People often ask Fe if he is afraid of becoming suicidal again. He says he has to be vigilant over this own thinking. He has to be willing to ask for help. Being in relationship with people who are part of the team that does this work is important for him to stay whole. He has learned the early warning signs that this is a path that I can't go down.

Fe says, "Most of us were delivered from the darkness and saved from our own self-destruction by experience of the love of God that came our way in flesh and blood human beings." He continues, "When we know that God is with us (not against us) through the presence of a compassionate community, our chances of surviving the night and entering a second day infinitely improves. People in the night are in unbelievable, unbearable pain. They may not be able to reach out to you for help. They need you to reach out to them."

Barbara Gulbranson

Affirmation

Everything I do is with a feeling of compassion for all beings. My heart is open, tender and completely loving.

Chapter Six

Bask in the Joy of Forgiveness

"Forgiveness is the fragrance that the violet sheds on the heel that has crushed it."
— MARK TWAIN

Forgiveness is the ultimate form of love. It is a total demonstration of kindness to ourselves and others. To forgive others, we must also forgive ourselves for anything we have done, either intentionally or unintentionally, that hurt someone else or any part of creation. To forgive people who act hurtful, cruel, insensitive, immature, selfish or completely disrespectful to your needs—to have forgiveness and compassion for these people—means journeying deep within to find that place where the Divine lives, breathes, and has its being. We must immerse ourselves in God's light that shines within us and radiates out to others. If we do this, our ability to forgive greatly increases. Instead of holding grudges, resentments, and anger toward one who has harmed us either emotionally or physically, we can open our hearts, allow ourselves to feel the pain, and move through the experience to a place that is loving, compassionate, and kind.

To transform ourselves, we must first understand that lack of forgiveness is like poison. It is much like a gaping open wound that festers into infection, turning joy into bitterness and happiness into vengeance. Failing to forgive keeps unwanted negative energies bottled up inside of us, festering and waiting to show up later as something worse like a life-threatening illness. We suffer through lack of forgiveness, trapped by the negativity in our consciousness and convinced that we have been victimized. Failing to forgive strangles the heart, depriving it of the ever-flowing river of love. Holding onto wrongdoings of others, whether intentional or unintentional, places a stronghold on our hearts and prevents healing in mind, body, and spirit. When we are unforgiving, we are not doing anything to the other person; instead, we are mentally torturing ourselves, blocking our full engagement in all the goodness and beauty that life has to offer. We see the perpetrator of our misery as the enemy or a monster and respond with vindictiveness, bitterness, and resentment.

The good news is that we can erase the ill effects of unforgiveness and can transform from a state of toxicity to one of positivity. If we can learn to forgive, we can be free from toxic states of mind such as anger, disappointment, misery, aggravation, guilt, agony, and frustration. We can break free from the shackles of unforgiveness that bind and restrict our hearts from fully living life.

We each have a choice. We can allow an experience of cruelty, betrayal, or abandonment make us tender and loving people, or we can allow it to make us callous and hard-hearted. By not forgiving, we are literally held captive by how someone else behaved and, as a result, we are continuously going over the past in our minds and not living in the present moment.

It reminds me of the ancient story of the prisoner. A prisoner was kept in a dungeon day after day, night after night. One night the prisoner got an idea. He decided he could no longer sustain living this way and he planned to break out of the cell. He went up the creepy, crumbly stairs to the door, readying himself to hit the guard on the head when he entered to deliver bread and water. As the prisoner practiced his escape, he touched the prison door handle. Amazingly, the door opened and sunlight streamed into his eyes. The prisoner walked out of the dungeon right past the guard to freedom. He was free all along and only held prisoner by his mindset.

The process of forgiving involves reframing our thinking, letting go, releasing the pain, and responding with love. A shift in consciousness is required in order to view the so-called enemy as someone who is suffering themselves, longing for love, and healing just the way we are. If we can stay in unitive consciousness, in this spiritually mature attitude, we can see that the Divine resides in this transgressor as well as in us. God lives in everyone alike, regardless of how the human mind judges, or should I say misjudges, another. This is eloquently stated in 1 Corinthians 3:16: "Do you not know that you are the temple of God and that the Spirit of God dwells in you?" Since we are each part of the whole, all aspects of the one God, when we send ill will to someone else, we are bringing it upon ourselves as well. Some call that the Law of Attraction, others call it karma or cause-and-effect. The bottom line is that divinity resides in each one of us alike and when we really integrate this truth into our consciousness, only then can we revere all of life and receive the most beautiful heartfelt posture of a forgiving nature. Where the pain once lived, love and compassion can now reside.

An example from my own life is when the friend who abandoned me came to me one year later, asking for forgiveness. While I verbalized forgiveness, I still held onto unexpressed anger and grief in my heart. When I later built the resolve to let it go, it felt like a part of me had died, which then enabled me to birth something new and wonderful. A newer, gentler, softer, more loving version of me was born and moved to fulfilling a life purpose of helping wounded hearts heal. This was a beautiful gift arising from the depths of sorrow. Often, as in my case, the letting go is a quiet movement of the heart with no fanfare—just a tender release of tainted energy that is now replaced with pure inner peace and quiet joy. From that place in the heart the gift can be borne. Once free, these feelings are not necessarily banished forever, but we can learn to consider our unforgiving feelings when they arise, recognize they are there, and let them go. When we see a lack of forgiveness smoldering within us, we can thank it for coming up to foster growth without reacting or getting hooked by it.

Doorway to Freedom

We are prisoners when we are unforgiving, but the doorway to freedom is always open for us to step out and release the chains of the past. Of course, forgiving does not mean that we plan violence to break away, and it doesn't mean we sustain abuse or mistreatment. It means that we release the power that the negative behavior holds on us by letting go of anger, resentment, hatred or vengeful plots, all of which cause us great harm physically, emotionally, and spiritually. By bringing lovingkindness to the forefront of our minds, we can change an unforgiving nature to a compassionate one. Simply set the intention of lovingkindness for yourself and others. Say,

I forgive all intentional and unintentional hurt that was aimed at me and intend to help all other people be free from pain.

Forgiveness is not a sign of weakness nor an attitude of rolling over and letting someone walk on you. It is instead a virtue that requires courage and strength. Mahatma Gandhi said, "The weak can never forgive. Forgiveness is an attribute of the strong." A forgiving nature peels away layers of resistance, opening channels of love, empathy, and compassion. All of life's experiences, including the ones that crack our hearts open wide, invite us to love each other in a deeper and more meaningful way.

None of us can escape the fact that someone will hurt us at some point in our lives. That doesn't mean we hide or seclude ourselves from others. We need to live life fully, and when we are hurt remind ourselves to return to that place in our hearts where the Divine lives to know we are loved; as a result, we can extend love and kindness even toward those who hurt us.

A Forgiveness Practice

To practice the art of forgiving, think back to a time when someone hurt you. You can review the story line but don't dwell on it. Instead, remember the feelings that you experienced. Don't deny them, just bring them gently to your mind. Now inhale and exhale slowly and connect to Spirit within you; tap into that vast expanse of love. Maybe you tap into that Source within you with a prayer, a feeling, or an affirmation. Recognize the Divine Presence within you that is always waiting for you to touch into it. Say silently or out loud, "I forgive you." Realize that you no longer need to hold on to the experience. Just let it go. Know that behind the smokescreen of your feelings is a spiritual purpose, a deeper meaning. You are now ready to gather whatever growth came from this process and release your hold on your negative feelings of hurt. Next, bless the experience and let it go. Allow God's peace to permeate your entire being and bask in it. Another meaningful way to shift your energy to a forgiving nature is to practice the Buddhist lovingkindness meditation described in Chapter 9.

No matter how painful an experience is, it can be a catalyst for growing greater love in your heart. You don't have to forget what happened or erase it from your mind if you shift your energy from negativity to lightness. By forgiving, you stay neutral when thoughts of a negative experience arise rather than reacting with intense negative emotion. The next time someone intentionally or unintentionally causes you pain, you will be empowered to tap into the well of love within you and can embrace the blessing of happiness that comes from a forgiving heart. Why? Because your ability for happiness decreases as your inability to forgive increases.

As much as we don't want to admit it, struggles help us discover our strength and inner beauty. An experience may be excruciatingly painful, but forgiving expands us as spiritual beings and we can bring us to a softer and gentler state. The Divine Lover beckons you to forgive, release, and respond with love. Expansion of the heart through Divine Love results in love flourishing in personal relationships.

Say:

> *I forgive, release and respond with love. I recognize that the Spirit that dwells in me dwells in you too. I unceasingly give the endless love and light that God has for me to others.*

Kindness in Action

If from our woundedness we forgive, we generate healing in ourselves and those who have hurt us. One poignant real-life example of this is illustrated in Rev. Patti's experience.

When Patti was fourteen years old, her elderly father arranged for her to be married to an older man. Her mother was in a state hospital at the time, which is why Patti's dad, who wanted to prevent the children from going to an orphanage, thought it would be a good idea to marry her to this man who offered to take care of Patti and her brother. Patti and the older man, Robbie, were married and moved from rural Maine to Massachusetts. After a few weeks, Robbie insisted she dress up and said, "I'm taking you out." However, instead of taking her to a restaurant or show as she'd hoped, he took his young and innocent wife to a brothel. He put her in a prostitute's room and came back with two other guys. He told her, "Make love to them to get some money." Patti tried to resist, crying, "No, I'm scared!" But they wouldn't let her go. The men raped her. At the first opportunity, Patti escaped out the back door but two men grabbed her, put her in the backseat of a car, locked the doors, and took off with her into the night.

Patti remembers that she ended up in a big gravel pit on a woodsy old dirt road. Her memories of the events remain hazy, but she recalls the men smoked and drank, and she remembers the smell of cigarettes, liquor, and maybe drugs. Three men (her husband was not one of them) raped and beat her throughout this time. She screamed and tried to get away, and they responded by beating her until she was in dreadful shape. At times the men would leave and come back an hour or so later. When they left, they tied her hands and feet to the backseat of the car doors. She tried to get up but couldn't. This went on for days.

On the third day, two of the men walked down the road to get cigarettes and liquor, leaving one man behind to watch Patti. The man left to watch Patti lit a cigarette, then looked into the backseat window of the car where she sat, crumpled and beaten. All of a sudden his face flooded with tears and he said, later, "All I could see in that backseat was what looked like a little bird that had died—when birds die they have that skeletal look and look awful." He recalls that he couldn't stop crying. He picked her up, carried her to the police station, and left her on the steps. As he started to leave, he saw a Unity church across the street and, for reasons he himself didn't understand, went in and sat through the service that was going on. When the service ended, the man sat still in the pew, feeling like he couldn't get up. The pastor came to his side, sat down, and put his arm around the man, who was crying. The man told the pastor what had happened and that he wanted to turn himself in but was afraid. The reverend went with him to the police station. Soon afterward, Patti was sent to her mother-in-law's home and was then transported back to her father's home in Maine.

More than twenty years later, when Patti was living in Florida, she attended a class on forgiveness at a church of Religious Science (Religious Science is a New Thought faith tradition founded by Dr. Ernest Holmes, much like Unity Church of Christianity). While reading the assigned book, everything came flooding back to her and she became so scared she couldn't get off the couch. But Patti knew she had to continue with the forgiveness class.

A week or two after beginning the class, Patti was in a restaurant with her friends when she noticed an old man staring at her. Patti said his staring "felt creepy." Hobbling with a cane, the man came over to her table and said, "You don't know me."

She replied, "No I don't. What do you want?"

With tears streaming down his face, the man answered, "I'd like to talk with you alone." Patti and the man went to another table and he said, "You have not changed, although you have weight on and are older. Your face is the same. I've been looking for you for years, hoping I would find you. I have to ask your forgiveness." The man went on, "I'm one of the men who raped and abused you when you were a little girl. I'm the one who took you to the police station." He continued, "I laid you down on the ground and went over to Unity Church and I stayed at the meeting and talked to the pastor and turned myself in. I spent a few months in jail and turned in the other two guys as well." He added, "I attend a church here in Florida and am taking a class on forgiveness. I knew when I took that class I felt that I would be forgiven for all because that is what I need before I leave the planet."

It turns out that the man was taking precisely the same class as Patti, only at another church. Patti said she was a Christian Science nurse and when she told him she was taking the same class, he turned white. A few days later, she saw the man again and was able to let go of the whole thing. She says she "felt all you should feel when you heal from something." She was able to forgive him. They talked on the phone and stayed in touch. He dedicated the rest of his life to Unity faith and God, and died three weeks later. Patti is certain that this man needed forgiveness to leave the planet.

Patti says that the man understood forgiveness was a lesson he needed to learn. She was the victim and he was the abuser. She says, "Universal law does take care of victims and abusers no matter what goes on. It's there for a purpose for a lesson to be learned on both sides." Patti teaches, "Whenever anybody hurts you, turn it around and look for the good you see in that person. There's good in everyone, no matter what they have done. They may appear evil and [have] done horrific acts, but you will find somewhere, if you look hard enough, even [by] a sparkle in the eye you can find beauty in everybody and everything, but you have to look deep."

She says, "I have always done that and stood by it. If you can't find an inkling of good, you can't forgive. Sometimes it's like baby steps, teeny teeny. For yourself and healing of everyone involved, you've got to look beyond what happened—that leads to loving people—and know this is only an experience... [realizing] the pain they must be going through themselves to be a rapist or killer, you can't think of the person without thinking, 'Boy, they must be in a lot of pain, physically or mentally.'"

As Patti explains, the man had a breakthrough when he was looking in the car window. He was a vicious man and a rapist. When he saw her as a small sparrow, a visual given from Spirit, he felt compassion and knew he had to get her out of there. Divine Mind shifted his consciousness. Compassion overwhelmed the whole situation. He knew he had to get her out of there. It was divine—literally—that all the resources he needed were nearby, visible and accessible to him. Patti concludes she "feels the experience was for him more than anything else."

Affirmation

*I forgive, release,
and respond with love.*

Chapter Seven

Survive the Terrible Twos

"When the consciousness is kept on God, you will have no fears; every obstacle will then be overcome by courage and faith."
— PARAMAHANSA YOGANANDA

"Holding onto anger is like grasping a hot coal with the intent of throwing it at someone else; you are the one who gets burned."
— BUDDHA

Fear and anger are called the terrible twos because they can derail a move toward kindness and create suffering in the individual. The claws of fear do not allow love and compassion to prevail because, when scared, you are too busy running or keeping your head above water to extend compassion and love not only to yourself but to others as well. Often fear is considered the opposite of love. Anger is the second part of the terrible twos. We all get angry at times. While anger can disempower us, spark emotional disturbances, and render us unable to help others, it can cause us to lean into negativity and consider only what is happening at the moment.

Instead of seeing the terrible twos as hurdles to triumph over, we can see them as transforming moments—moments to use for spiritual awakening. We can fuel the fear and anger by getting caught up in the drama, or we can step aside from the drama, look it squarely in the face, thank it for coming, and use it as another stepping stone on the spiritual path we are walking. Both anger and fear afford us opportunities to increase compassion for ourselves and others.

The Face of Fear

Everyone feels fear at one time or another. In New Thought, it is said that fear arises when you feel separate from God. In truth, you can never be separated from God, the Source of your being. Nothing triggers fear as much as the made-up stories in our heads. Our minds are proficient at creating all kinds of frightening scenarios. Often fear comes up and it is for something that hasn't even happened and most likely won't ever happen. We start imagining all sorts of scenarios and our minds run wild with story lines in which the main attraction is loss. For example, your teenager is out late at night and you think something awful has happened. You decide your boss is plotting against you and you're going to lose your job. Maybe you have a medical test done and you've crafted a terminal disease as the only outcome. You become jealous of someone else and fear you will lose your relationship. In recent times, there's fear surrounding the victory of a political candidate and what that means to our society regarding women's rights, the environment, taxes, and human rights. Other popular fears are public speaking, bugs, heights and loneliness. The number one fear in America is public speaking and the number five fear is death. Interestingly, while many people fear death, most of the hospice patients I worked with don't have this fear and are comfortable with, and even welcoming of, the physical release of a body that is no longer functioning for them.

Usually fear has to do with dreading loss of any kind. Loss of life. Loss of material possessions. Loss of a relationship. Loss of a job. Loss of health. Loss of social standing. Fear of loss has to do with attachment to that which is impermanent. That fear is one of the root causes of suffering. In addition to fearing loss, we become afraid when we feel we are no longer in control when facing, for example, a terminal disease, an unwanted divorce, a loved one dying or a natural disaster that destroys our home. Whatever fear you have, it means you are not feeling aligned with the Divine Presence within. There is an emptiness—a complete abandonment of your faith in a universal power of good.

Because we are human, fear will continue to crop up. In fact, fear is wired into our humanness. All of humanity and the animal kingdom instinctively respond to a threat with fear. Often, the survival of a species depends on this reaction to a threat. It's important to note that fear crops up from deep within us in response to an outer stimulus, often causing a knee-jerk reaction. This is why common acronym for FEAR is Forget Everything And Run. Yet spiritually grounded people can respond to fear stimuli with a calm center of peace because they are unattached to the outcome and unattached to form whether it be human form or material possessions. We can learn to live our lives fully and freely despite fear.

It is important to note that fear can be the catalyst for advancing on our spiritual path. It's a chance to transform ourselves and enliven a greater sense of self. Fear is natural when you are growing and stretching the envelope, so to speak. Say, for example, you accept that promotion at work which will entail growth on your part. Or you have a speaking engagement in front of a large audience and your knees are shaking while walking over to the podium. Perhaps you just had a baby and you are fearful of whether or not you will be able to keep the child safe and nurtured. This is productive fear which serves us well because it is the impetus to growth and expansion. We can accept the heavenly invitation to grow even with the presence of fear, or stay stagnant because fear can keep us immobilized.

An example of fear from my own life took place during a minister's retreat in Arizona. I was invited to participate in a sweat lodge and I said yes without even knowing what it was. The sweat lodge was run by a shaman in an impossibly small tent with hot coals in the middle. My group was not allowed to leave the tent for 90 minutes and it was sweltering hot. Worse yet, I get claustrophobic in close quarters and thought I was going to die. "Please let me out," I begged the shaman. Her answer was a firm no. I was so afraid that I felt my heartbeat quicken and felt faint. In the midst of this fear, my little finger found its way under the tent to the outside air. The shaman did ask where the small slit of light was coming from but fortunately dropped the subject. With my pinky finger outside of the tent, I felt comforted that freedom and fresh air awaited me. During the ceremony, the shaman gave each of us Indian names. Surprisingly, mine was "fearless finch." As the ceremony progressed, something inside me shifted and I felt a deep compassion for the others in my group and, eventually, for all the animals and humans in the world. I felt deep gratitude for all of life. I was renewed and felt uplifted and transformed as a result of the experience. Instead of running from fear, like we so often do, I was forced to stay with it and be in the moment with it.

The sweat lodge was a stimulus of fear for me but may not be for another person. Fear comes in all shapes and sizes, depending on what it is that you respond to in this way. Even so, fear is an impetus to bring us closer to spiritual teachings. With the experience of fear is the opportunity to exhibit faith—that the Divine Presence is always within us and we can never be separated from it no matter what peril, real or imagined, we face. Standing tall in the face of fear requires courage. Courage doesn't mean that we don't feel fear; it means we can use it to move forward in our spiritual development.

Out of Fear

We get wrapped up in fear for all sorts of reasons. Maybe it is the employee evaluation you are having tomorrow. Perhaps it is watching your child take that first school bus ride to kindergarten. Maybe it's taking a chance on a relationship and feeling vulnerable that you may get hurt. When fear arises, our culture tells us to pop the latest pill and deaden our natural response to such situations.

Some of us turn to food, drink, or substance abuse to alleviate the symptoms of fear. None of these are adequate remedies. An effective response for fear is to feel your feelings when they arise. Stay with the feelings and don't brush them aside. Remember that fear has been your bane all these years and now it's time to shift to a new level of consciousness. Just remember the Divine Presence is ever enfolding you in love. Have the courage and faith to allow life to unfold and to empty yourself of fear. Be willing to listen to the message fear is giving you and let it teach you what you need to learn. When fear arises, stop and be still. And breathe. Just be with the feeling and experience it as it happens. Our humanity calls for us to feel our feelings and we shouldn't label them as "good" or "bad." They just are. Be in the present moment with fear and use it as an impetus for shift. Don't empower it to overwhelm you.

While fear will crop up occasionally because it is part of the human experience, you have the power to switch from terror to a deep, abiding peace because you are always connected to God and always connected to your source of all good. Remember that you are never separated from God who dwells within you, and don't forget to live in the present moment. Think of the animal kingdom. The animals—dogs, cats, wolves, bears, bees, birds, raccoons, sea life—all live in the present moment. Nature can't reason and has no idea of future dangers. What sidetracks us humans is fearing what will happen in the coming days, months, years. If this happens, bring your attention back to the present moment and stay there without projecting out to the future.

Say:

> I am always connected to God and always connected to my good. Love casts out fear. My heart swells with love for my creator and creation.

Working with Anger

Anger is classified as one of the terrible twos because of its destructive nature. Anger arises when we feel someone has done us wrong, whether that is true or imagined. Anger stems from hurt and sadness, and is especially destructive when, as it often does, it leads to physical and emotional damage to those who bear the brunt of our anger. You are not a bad person for feeling angry; it's part of the human experience. Getting angry, however, stops the flow of peace and well-being, and disconnects us from compassion by causing us to dehumanize the person we are angry at. We see them not as a human with feelings just like ours, but as monsters devoid of feelings, which can lead to severe consequences.

Despite this, anger can sometimes be the catalyst for great change in the world. When enough people are angry about our environment, world hunger, war, dangerous drugs, animal extinction, and other universal issues, change results. During those instances, anger can be productive as long as the measures to carry out change are peaceful.

However, when anger is fueled by judgment and vengeance, it ceases to be productive and has the opposite effect. Think for moment of a love relationship. All is going well until one partner believes the other did something wrong—some type of hurt, disagreement, or betrayal. The love is instantly diminished and physical and verbal abuse can shake the foundation of the relationship. Our speech stemming from anger can cause great harm to someone else. Saying "I'm sorry" doesn't always erase the negative effects that reside in the hurt person's subconscious mind derailing trust and innocence.

It's impossible to have love and compassion for others while you are harboring anger at another for some real or imagined offense. Yet all this pain and suffering is not necessary. We can, and must, release it if we are going to become loving, kind, and compassionate. I am not suggesting that you repress anger because that in and of itself is detrimental to health and well-being. We need to recognize our anger before we explode and learn to live in the space between the arising of anger and the explosion of it. In that space, take a moment to see the anger rearing its head. Instead of letting it erupt, take a few deep breaths. You might want to wish every being on earth who is experiencing anger, patience, and peace by saying: *May all beings have patience. May all beings have peace.* Now let peace move through you and although anger has shown up, which is part of being human, it has been disarmed from harming anyone.

I can call to mind a time when I was terribly angry. My father had recently passed away and I was having his mail forwarded to my address. Somehow companies got hold of his so-called new address and instead of getting forwarded mail, I was getting mail directly sent to him at my address. One popular furniture company sent him

Authentic Kindness

an entire catalog of furnishings with a greeting, "Welcome to the neighborhood!" While grieving my dad's passing and settling his affairs, it came as a blow for some company to send him greetings to his new neighborhood. A wave of fiery emotion washed over me, Grabbing the phone, I immediately called this company's customer service department ready to give them a piece of my mind. Somehow I was able to catch myself between the moment of outrage and the full volcanic eruption. I caught myself and just breathed into the moment. I asked myself, "What would kindness do?" I relaxed into the sensations and by the time the customer-service representative picked up the phone, I was able to speak kindly and explain the matter and request my dad's name be removed from the mailing list. In turn, I was met with compassion by the person on the other end of the phone and realized deep in my heart there was no need to lash out at her. Although I allowed myself to feel the emotion, I did not let it hurt myself or anyone else. We really need to get that it's okay to feel your feelings, but to not let them take you away from compassion; that is the key.

Anger comes from inside you. It is not the situation that causes anger. It is the situation that triggered what is already dormant inside of you, and that same trigger presented to another person may not cause anger at all. Think for a moment of this scene:

You are rushing around in a shopping mall with little time to make your purchases. You are stressed and hurrying and someone bumps into you and all your packages spill to the ground. You respond with anger, cussing at the person while your blood is boiling as a result of the nasty inconvenience. Now take the same situation where you are shopping and someone bumps into you. However, you are not in a rush and not stressed on this lovely day. Someone bumps into you and all your packages spill to the ground. As you gather up the packages, you smile at the person and say, "No problem." You see the incident is the same; it is you who reacts differently. Anger is an inside job and you are the one who reacts to a stimulus with anger or with love and compassion.

We all have experienced being in a car with someone who gets angry at all the other drivers. The driver is cussing at the other drivers for moving too slow, for being too close to the curb, for taking too long at a toll booth. This serves no purpose and only fuels the driver's unhappiness. Surely we can understand that this kind of negative response only makes us unhappy and stressed, and peace cannot live in a toxic state of mind.

The antidote to anger is to develop love and patience. So when you feel anger arising you don't have to deny it's there; instead, welcome its presence as an opportunity to make a new choice. Practice patience and love instead of anger and you will have a much different outcome of lashing out at someone in anger. One Buddhist practice is to remember that others all over the world are feeling the anger you are feeling right now and stop and send lovingkindness out to all these people who are experiencing what you are. You may want to practice the lovingkindness meditation described in Chapter 9. This is a powerful way of softening the heart and replacing anger with love, compassion, and patience.

Once you see the outcome of being loving instead of being angry, you will be more accustomed to reacting with patience and kindness than with anger; kindness will build upon itself until it is automatic to respond with love. You are replacing the habit of anger with a new habit—that of love and patience.

Kindness in Action

My former work as a hospice chaplain brought me to many nursing homes and memory care facilities. The memory care facilities are filled with people with Alzheimer's and dementia, in different stages, as well as skilled care givers who lovingly take care of the patients.

Many hospice Alzheimer's and dementia patients get angry at imagined scenarios due to their illness. Recognizing this, the owner of one of these beautiful facilities was particularly dedicated to creating a peaceful environment for residents. Knowing that one of the residents was a banker who thrived on going to work each day, the memory care facility owner brought in an old-timey wooden desk, typewriter, and telephone and set up an office front in the living area at his own expense. Each day, this resident happily goes to "work at the bank as usual" thanks to this sincere act of kindness by the owner.

Barbara Gulbranson

Affirmation

When angry I stop, breathe, and practice patience, love, and kindness. I feel peace permeating my entire being.

Chapter Eight

Cultivate Kindness

"Don't fight darkness. Bring the light, and the darkness will disappear. The power of light is always bigger than the power of darkness."
— MAHARISHI MAHESH YOGI

We are all hardwired to be compassionate. Compassion, love, and kindness are our natural states of being. All too often our abilities to be compassionate are hidden behind a veil of stress, strain, fear, anger, and worry. Despite this, God's light is within us all the time yearning to shine out from us to others. In the First Epistle of John, he says, "God is light, and in him there is no darkness at all" (1 John 1:5).

When we have fallen to the depths of darkness, we can develop deeper compassion to give kindness to others by allowing our inner light to blaze. Our goal, then, is not to find the light, but to allow it to shine from us because it is already there and can never be extinguished. In other words, when we perceive darkness, we should not try to dispel it, but merely turn on the light. When we embark of the path of compassion and kindness, there is no separation between us and the light of the Divine Presence within. There never was a separation. Only in our misguided attempts to live life from the human perspective instead of from the spiritual perspective had we allowed the light to dim, but it can never be separated from us or us from it.

We can uncover that light and allow it to blaze strongly from within us by serving others with lovingkindness. Our happiness is increased when we are in service to others with lovingkindness in our hearts. But how do we master the art of lovingkindness while living in a world that values material possessions, climbing the ladder of success, aggression, and engaging in destructive habits such as drinking and drug use, judging others, attachment, and greed?

A passage from the Chandogya Upanishad (III, 13, 7) reads, "The light which shines from beyond the sky, beyond the highest of the highest worlds, beyond everything that is, is in truth the same light that shines inside human beingness." Fear, worry, shame, hatred, guilt, greed, and judgment may dim the light but can never extinguish this eternal blaze within. For this is the light of the most high which forever shines within our beingness at a place where the human and Divine meet.

Egolessness

Egocentric people are without compassion. The ego bullies us and relishes in getting us to think that we are separate from ourselves and others. The ego announces in your mind that you are unworthy, unattractive, untalented, and unfit to succeed. It's the exact opposite of lovingkindness. For compassion and kindness to be born, we must develop egolessness. By dropping the ego, we can be kind to ourselves and others. Losing the ego cultivates an awareness of others and a move away from the "I" in everything you perceive. In this way, you develop empathy toward others. Typically, we are so focused on "I" and "mine" that we don't have space to help others. By losing the "I," we open a wide expanse to help others. What a relief to lose the ego. You revel in the peace and freedom this brings and become a tender and compassionate person. Losing the ego activates kindness toward yourself and others. You stop the fixation with "myself" and once that is released, your innate kindness toward others blossoms.

You don't need any special invitation to drop the ego; anyone can do it by setting the intention in mind. Egolessness comes from dropping your agenda of "What's in it for me?" Shifting your attention to "How can I help others?" empowers egolessness to take center stage in your life. It becomes the new norm.

When we see only the "I," we are living in duality consciousness because we don't see that we are all interconnected. The ego is the one who is boasting, "Look at me. I'm so great. I did this wonderful thing." But it is not about us. We are not the actors, so we don't get a standing ovation for success. It is God working through us as an instrument of expression. For example, when I write a book, it is not me who is doing the work. I understand that it is God within me using me as a vehicle of expression. Therefore, I take no ownership in this because it is God's and it is my pleasure to be an instrument of Spirit. Before I sit down to write, I affirm that God, the ascended masters and angels, are doing this work by means of me. Then I let go. I affirm the following:

Barbara Gulbranson

I give myself over to God and the angels to write this book by means of me. I allow divine messages to come through me to go out to heal the hearts and souls of many.

There is simply no need to inflate oneself when doing God's work. We can be humble instruments of Spirit working successfully through us. We can understand that our Creator is our partner in all of life and in our work as well. We are not the author of what we do: God is the author.

To obliterate the ego, we want to start out by simply observing it at work. Whenever we want to take credit for something, boast, inflate, exaggerate, criticize or retaliate, it's the ego running the show. If people annoy or criticize you, you want to get back at them and prove how wonderful you truly are. But this is counterproductive with the value of compassion toward yourself and others. When retaliatory urges arise, becoming aware of them is the first step in changing your reaction to the negative stimulus. Then refocus your energy constructively and give the situation to God. Soon it will become natural to release the ego's stronghold on your mind and to live humbly as an instrument of God. You will feel great joy and love as your heart and soul opens up in this way.

A beautiful verse in the Bhagavad Gita XIII:7–11 (excerpted from *The Yoga of Jesus* by Paramahansa Yogananda)[1] describes the human who has shed the ego, who remains even in all situations and who has attained unitive consciousness:

"(The sage is marked by) humility, lack of hypocrisy, harmlessness, forgiveness, uprightness, service to the guru, purity of mind and body, steadfastness, self-control;

Indifference to sense objects, absence of egotism, understanding of the pain and evils (inherent in mortal life): birth, illness, old age, and death;

Nonattachment, nonidentification of the Self with such as one's children, wife, and home: constant equal-mindedness in desirable and undesirable circumstances;

Unswerving devotion to Me by the yoga of nonseparativeness, resort to solitary places, avoidance of the company of worldly men;

Perseverance in Self-knowledge; and meditative perception of the object of all learning—the true essence or meaning therein. All these qualities constitute wisdom; qualities opposed to them constitute ignorance."

Equanimity

For many of us, our emotions are up and down. Something triggers us and down we go feeling resentful, hurt, stressed, or outraged. By contrast when something pleasant occurs we go up feeling happy, giddy, and on top of the world. In any given day our emotions jump around and bounce from feeling to feeling. There is a way to mitigate the swings of our emotions. By developing even-mindedness, which is a balanced state of evenness, we walk the path to peace of mind.

All too often people think that even-mindedness means that you are apathetic—that you don't care. Quite the opposite is true. With an even mind, we care deeply for others yet remain unaffected by the story line or the outcome. Even-mindedness, or equanimity, is so essential to reaching higher levels of consciousness that the Buddhists consider it one of the four limitless ones. The four limitless ones, taken as a group, are what Buddhists believe herald in the awakening of the enlightened heart. Buddhist teacher and author Paul Rinpoche explains it like this: "We can summarize the four boundless qualities in the single phrase, 'a kind heart.' Just train yourself to have a kind heart always and in all situations."

When looking at the limitless ones, we start with what we have in a limited form. For example, it is limited to love one particular person or just your family members and friends. Most of us start with living life through a limited lens, yet the potential is unlimited. We begin by loving one person, which is personal love; sometimes this is romantic love. Then by cultivating a higher consciousness, we develop the unlimited capacity to love, which is universal love. Now we have expanded our capacity to love and feel compassion for everyone, and our heart and mind opens up to everyone—no matter who someone is or what they may have done. Our goal is to have unconditional love for all of creation, even for the most difficult people in our lives or in the world. Being of even mind, we achieve lovingkindness.

Authentic Kindness

Our goal, then, is to stay even-minded in the face of adversity. We keep our sense of calm and deep abiding joy no matter what is going on around us. We simply stop, look at what we are feeling, and catch the mind before it falls into extreme thinking. This is how we free ourselves from aggression and experience an evenness or stability. We don't get debilitated when things go up and down, as in life they will. We remain as a calm center in the face of the storm. That doesn't mean the storm is not happening. It means we stay calm no matter what chaos or turmoil is going on around us.

For example, imagine that you are pulling out of parking space and you bump into a parked vehicle. There is damage to your car but none to the car you hit. You come home and your husband or wife gets angry at you and calls you "stupid" for the accident. If you are even-minded, you are able to remain calm even while someone is hurling insults at you. By the same token, let's foresee your spouse as complimenting you and telling you how accomplished you are for something you have done. In the ideal state of equanimity, the praise doesn't make you conceited. That's because, in an even-minded state, you won't require compliments for your happiness and you sincerely will not be looking for personal gain.

When we are even-minded, we simply don't get caught up in whatever is happening. It's all even. Our hearts may remain open in any situation and not go to extremes or become reactionary; nothing throws us for a loop. We can therefore remain joyous even when difficult times arise. In fact, sometimes in the heart of a discouraging situation, the greatest love can be found. There's freedom in knowing we can feel calm and centered no matter what life throws at us. We can remain in the highest state of the Infinite Bliss mode of action. With a still mind, we are fully present in whatever is occurring in our lives. The peace that is deep in your inner being is not dependent on things going well in the world of cause-and-effect. Uncovering this peace entails a willingness to go into the fray and experience the stings of life that can disturb us to our core, but perhaps some of these trials arise to break us free from attachment to the world of form. As a result of the process, we forge a deeper connection with Spirit and with humanity by meeting others and life's circumstances right where they are.

When I worked for hospice people would ask me how I can do this work without getting attached to the patients. With equanimity you can help a friend, stranger, enemy or loved one with an equalized state of mind without strong attachments to others. That doesn't mean you are devoid of feelings or lack empathy. Rather, it means losing strong attachments and refraining from clinging to others while still loving another unconditionally. One of the best tests of equanimity occurs when we feel proud of ourselves for helping someone else we really went out of our way to help and receive no gratitude from that person, who maybe even expresses rejection and downright resentfulness toward our efforts. To remain unruffled in this situation is a challenging test of our mastery of the even-minded state of being. We can thus monitor our progress by our true inner reactions to this type of situation.

An example of a challenge test of equanimity states is Brett's kindness story, at the end of this chapter. Brett's experience is an example of the triumph of compassion coupled with love and even-mindedness. To remain calm and balanced, and accept whatever comes just as it is, is to be free. We can allow life to unfold through us and around us and maintain a deep abiding joy that comes from letting go of outcomes or demanding that a situation look a certain way. Developing equanimity is a sacred gift. We become comfortable with life however it unfolds and even see calamity as an opportunity to express greater patience and compassion. Now we are in the Divine Flow of life, not resisting but allowing ourselves to be at peace in whatever takes place.

Being even-minded begins with the intention to stop clinging to form or to the outcome of a situation. Have faith that life enfolds exactly as it should instead of resisting life and demanding that events turn out a certain way. Quietly surrender to what is happening and meet the situation–no matter how harsh it is–with love and understanding. Have calm confidence, knowing that whatever life brings is a call for expansion of your heart and consciousness. All you need to do is keep an even mind and not get tossed around like a ship sailing on stormy seas. The next time you are challenged with a disturbing situation in your life—whether someone cuts you off in traffic, pushes in front of you on line at the store, or tries to engage you in an argument—I invite you to maintain an even mind to see how differently you feel by extinguishing the flame of indignation or rage. Watch as the love grows in your heart and expands wider than ever before. I assure you that the deep abiding joy you will feel from being even-minded is a blessing for you as you walk this sacred path toward enlightenment.

Generosity

One of the most effective ways of deepening one's compassion for others is by cultivating a generous nature. Generosity is giving of oneself in a pure form without strings attached. It is the total opposite of poverty thinking. It is realizing that we live in an abundant universe and there's great joy in sharing what you have with others, whether it is a material gift or a intangible gift from the heart such as love, compassion, empathy, understanding, and patience. Giving is a powerful spiritual strength and once you start doing it, the desire to give strengthens. Another benefit of giving is that it frees us from attachment and aligns us with the abundant universe. Many sages take vows to never own anything. The Dharma Jord Jamsar put it this way: "Since I don't have the slightest feeling that I am the owner of my belongings, someone who takes them away can hardly be a thief."

Much like unconditional love we give without expecting anything in return, we give because we want to. It's not an obligation or a technique to get others to like us. We can be generous because the universe is plentiful and the reservoir of our good can never run dry. In understanding this, we are able to open up and give everything. Generosity benefits others greatly and cultivates compassion. While we don't give with the goal of receiving, we receive feelings of well-being and joy as we give to others. Giving brings happiness each time it is expressed. We experience joy in forming the intention to give, we experience joy in the act of giving, and we experience joy in remembering that we have given. Buddha said that if we knew, as he did, the power of giving, we would not let a single meal pass without sharing some of it. St. Francis of Assisi put it this way: "For it is in the giving that we receive."

Unfortunately, most of us are attached to form, which causes suffering. That's because we are continually seeking the next material thing, another person's affections, or whatever it is we desire. When we are attached to something, we tend to guard it, hold on tight to it, and not give it away. This, in turn, creates stress because form is always changing and no matter how hard we try, we can't stop change. Once we have the desired item, we begin seeking again, so this cycle never ends. It's never enough. Yet as we grow in consciousness, it finally sinks in that form is impermanent. Finally, we drop clinging to form and we are set free.

We are able to develop generosity when we are free from the clutches of clinging to form and, rather, we exist in the Divine flow and embrace the changing nature of life. Generosity goes beyond giving someone a particular item; it includes the giving of love, kindness, compassion, and empathy. Within our inner being lies generosity. Expressing a generous nature for ourselves and others sets us free and opens the gateway to deep love and joy.

Developing a generous nature is accomplished not by thinking through what might be generous to do, but by raising your consciousness to higher levels. Instead of saying, "I should be generous," go out and *be* generous—give something to somebody, whether it is a smile, empathy, love, or a precious material possession. As you move through your week, I invite you to give something away every day. You can start with family members and friends if you are most comfortable doing so, but then extend generosity out to people you don't know and who are not in your inner circle. It requires real detachment from what is termed form to let go of a prized possession. However, you can do this and trust that we do not live in a scarce universe; there is an unlimited supply of good for you. The abundance of the universe will never run out. When you are poised with a generous nature, you will feel your heart and soul open wide. When you give, you will receive many times over in terms of peace, love, and joy.

    I remember a time from my own life where I learned the virtue of generosity. My siblings and I were in the midst of selling my deceased father's condo when his former girlfriend got the key to his home from his roommate and stole his big-screen television along with other personal items. She wrote the children an email claiming that she deserved these items and meant to sell them at a garage sale. I was extremely angry not just that she took some of the only things I had to remind me of my father, but that she didn't want them because of a heartfelt need to have something to remember him by; she just wanted to profit monetarily. The anger was churning inside of me, gnawing at my stomach and growing like a forest fire. My verbal reaction included pronouncements of "Call the police" and "She needs to be locked up." I had to get hold of myself: if I called the police, I would be instrumental in sending a seventy-year-old woman to jail. What would that accomplish? I forced myself to recognize the anger for what it was and just sat in awareness of it. Then I consciously remembered the spiritual teachings that I live by. I took some deep breaths and prayed, and made the decision to practice generosity. Let her have the television and the other items. She obviously needs them more than we do. This experience was actually a blessing because it pushed my buttons so hard that I had to practice generosity or become enraged with all the physical and emotional suffering that would cause me and others. I remembered a Buddhist slogan I had just learned which shifted my energy away from anger to peace. It is verse three from *Thirty-Seven Practices of a Bodhisattva* by Tokme Zongpo:

> "Don't engage disturbances and emotional
> reactions fade away.
> Don't engage distractions and spiritual
> practice naturally grows.
> Keep awareness clear and vivid and
> confidence in the way arises.
> Rely on silence—this is the practice of a bodhisattva."

This slogan is especially helpful whenever you find yourself starting to react. It helps to memorize the verse and call it to mind when a disturbance arises. In my situation, it empowered me to still my racing mind and opt for generosity. As a result, the flames of rage were extinguished and peace permeated my being once again.

To this day, I can recall the experience and have no anger arise. I can live afresh the freedom that comes from practicing generosity.

Generosity doesn't have to be expressed in a grandiose gesture; often the smallest acts of giving bring the greatest rewards. This happened to me during a hospice chaplain call to a ninety-nine-year-old woman. When I arrived in her room, the patient was agitated because she said people were taking her things. Several items were missing from her room and she said people came in, went through her belongings, and took them. This was not the case at all but it was reality in her mind. Since the patient was hard of hearing, we often communicated by writing notes to each other. I pulled out my little spiral-bound notepad to write and she said, "That's mine. That's my notepad." My first reaction was to say, "No. This is my notepad. I use this pad for recording my mileage. See." Again, the patient insisted it was her notepad. In a flash, I realized that there was no benefit in proving her wrong or proving myself right. Instead I said, "Please, take this notepad. It's yours." And I handed it to her. She flipped through the pages and carefully looked at them. Then she said, "This isn't my notepad." I told her to keep the pad as a gift. When I left at the end of the visit, she thanked me over and over again for giving her the "book." It was I who should have thanked her for the opportunity to practice generosity. Even a small gesture like a notepad brings great pleasure to the one who is giving.

Another side effect of generosity is that once you cultivate it, gratitude flows. Gratitude springs from a heart that does not reside in lack but that recognizes that we are abundantly provided for. Gratitude is one of the most powerful positive energies in the universe. If we truly believe that God is in all and through all, we can be grateful for whatever we are experiencing. When I worked with terminally ill patients, I saw people who are grateful for a cup of coffee, a touch of the hand, a blanket placed on their lap, a prayer said with deep faith.

A Wall of Gratitude

When the now-deceased Claudia Mulcahy, author of *Cancer: What to Do or Say*, was diagnosed with stage-three breast cancer, within one week of that diagnosis she turned a wall in her living room into "The Wall of Gratitude." She wrote names, events, and things that she is grateful for each day in colorful felt-tip markers on shelf paper tacked on her living room wall "like wallpaper." When sharing about the Wall of Gratitude concept with other cancer patients, they all said that it took a newcomer to the group to point out something so uplifting, yet so easy. Reading the ongoing list of good aspects of her life lifted and thrills those who come to visit. Those who came shared their favorites and were genuinely touched in seeing their names on the list. Claudia said, "No matter how bad the day is, I can come up with something for which I'm grateful. There's a pony in this pile of poop! Stop whining. Get back to the Truth that life is good and it's a privilege." She tells us she uses various felt-tip pen colors to revisit the people, places, and events that fill her heart every day. She said, "It kept me focused on my good. There's so much kindness in the world. For this, I am grateful." Some of the notations include: "I love my hair. My smile. My eyebrows. My teeth. My weight. My neck. And I love you. You are all on my 'Wall of Gratitude.' So are the shade trees and Kleenex."

Yes, there is still physical pain and suffering in life, but you have a choice to live with a reverent appreciation of the whole of life or to complain and take a "woe is me" attitude. Instead of feeling sorry for yourself, start appreciating your grouchy spouse, a nitpicky boss, a stern teacher, or an irresponsible child. Appreciate the seemingly negative conditions along with the positive and beautiful ones. If people facing their darkest hours, like the patients I visited in hospice, can be grateful, you can too. Feel gratitude for something, whether it's a rainbow, your cat curled up in your lap, or a smile from a stranger until gratitude becomes your constant companion. It is, after all, your natural state of being.

Kindness in Action

Practicing equanimity is easy when others accept your lovingkindness, but can be challenging when you go all out for another person only to have your efforts rejected. This is precisely what happened to Midwesterner Brett when he tried to help a homeless man on a rainy day in Grand Central Station, New York.

After a long day of looking at a college for his daughter, Brett waited with his family in a crowd of disgruntled city people who were all waiting for access to a train platform to be opened. The New Yorkers were jostling and angling, periodically breaking away to sprint for various doors upon the announcement of train access times, when the family was approached by a disheveled middle-aged man. "Can you help me? I have identification, I'm homeless," he said, producing a card that looked like a driver's license.

"What do you need?" Brett asked immediately, barely glancing at the card.

"Everything," the main said.

"Food?"

"Yeah," the man replied, shrugging.

Brett hesitated: the man did not seem pleased by the offer, which was puzzling. Brett did not have cash left to hand the man, and he preferred to help people with food and conversation anyway. But the family was not from the city and his wife and daughter would be left without a lot of ways to reconnect with him if the access doors opened. He made a quick decision, calling, "I'll be back as soon as I can" as he followed the man out of the hall. His family waited in the same spot for him for anxious minutes, fearing that he wouldn't make it back in time, buffeted by bodies pushing past. Checking her watch after 10 minutes, his wife looked down... and, incredibly, straight at the homeless man. Fright overtook her upon seeing the man alone, working the crowd just a few people away from her. "Where's my husband?" she asked. He shrugged away, refusing to engage her, turning his back and asking people for "just money."

Just at that moment when her fear was at its height, Brett stepped through the crowd. "I don't know," he said, concern. "We left here and he was just about running I thought I'd lose him. We went so far I didn't have a clue about where we were or how I'd find my way back, and he stopped in front of a pizza store. He said he couldn't go in—something about a ban on homeless people—and sent me in for a pizza and soda. By the time I came out with them just a few minutes later, he was gone. I had to throw the food away to make it back here in time. I just feel so bad that I lost him."

Brett noticed the man and immediately focused concern on him, apologizing for throwing away the food and asking where the man went. "You ditched me! If I wasn't a nicer guy, I'd beat you up. I might just beat you up still. Or you can give me money." Thankfully and perhaps held in the protection of God, the access doors opened then and the crowds pushed the family out of harm's way and down to the train. Even as Brett boarded, he was troubled by the thought: *What else could I have done to help him?* The man was not grateful for Brett's actions or concern, which continued even as the man ditched him in unfamiliar territory and threatened his family's safety. This is the nature of lovingkindness—it is focused only on meaningful expression toward others.

Barbara Gulbranson

Affirmation

I let go of outcomes and see every situation as an opportunity to express patience, love, and compassion. Being in the Divine flow of life, I am at peace with whatever takes place.

Chapter Nine

Relax into the Simplicity of Being

"As you simplify your life, the laws of the universe will be simpler, solitude will not be solitude, poverty will not be poverty nor weakness weakness."
— HENRY DAVID THOREAU

I often think about how many of us are trading inner peace for busyness. Business meetings, appointments, conference calls, household chores, activities, computers, and cell phones keep us spinning round like a hamster in its wheel. We overschedule ourselves and make life more demanding than it has to be. It's not enough that we enslave ourselves to constantly doing, but many of us impose this on our children with endless activities that don't give the child a chance to simply be. It's no wonder a study conducted by the Centers for Disease Control (CDC) showed that, as of 2011, an estimated 6.4 million children ages four to seventeen have been diagnosed at some point with Attention-Deficit/Hyperactivity Disorder (ADHD) with drug prescriptions for approximately two-thirds of them. Sadly, we are ensnared in a fallacy that doing brings achievement, success, and happiness; as a result, we move away from peace by adding more and more stress onto our daily load.

Barbara Gulbranson

When life is hectic, we forget to pause and take in the wonder and magic of the world around us. We spend increasingly more time doing than simply being. We barely notice a beautiful sunset, the touch of a soft morning breeze, the song of a delightful bird, or the sweet fragrance of a rose in bloom. All of this overdoing creates stress and strain, makes life less enjoyable, robs us of our innate happiness, and leaves us too depleted for compassion to take root and grow in our inner being. Eventually we feel disconnected from our Source and forget that a life lived simply is the life that awakens spiritual majesty. We are here to allow God to express through us as love by giving our unique gifts to the world. When we are conscious of God working in us, as us and through us, the giving of these gifts can flow in an easy and effortlessly fashion. Overactivity holds us back from reaching higher states of consciousness and cultivating authentic kindness in our hearts. We must let go of our excessive activity levels to make room for compassion and kindness to grow.

The characteristics of someone living in simplicity include love, compassion, kindness, awareness, unitive consciousness, freedom from attachment, egolessness, even-mindedness, and courage. The person views the world with peace and harmony. This vantage point results from not only longing to give love and kindness to others, but also having the courage to do so based on the understanding that we are all one, and kindness opens the heart to greater dimensions in consciousness. Relationships then are not combative because the individual is not filled up with the distractions of the world but living from a much simpler point of view. This outpouring of love and compassion to others can only spring from a heart that has shed the dictates of the world and lives free from what our current culture defines as normal. When we move toward a simpler way of being, we accept the full power, glory, and grace of God. Our natural state is simple, marked by an absence of need for the superficial things that we may seek with cultural approval. Living simply does not mean sitting on the couch doing nothing. It means living to our full potential as a powerful cocreator with God. Now every experience we have is rooted in love and understanding, and we have the courage to practice generosity, forgiveness, self-kindness, and friendliness. Our ego is diminished and compassion is front and center in our consciousness. We see others as an extension of ourselves with the same feelings, desires, and fears that we have. We no longer see duality but the integration of you, me, and the universe.

Simplifying your life makes all this possible. A simplified life empowers you to have a transformed consciousness that springs from understanding the interconnectedness of all of life. If you take a few steps toward simplification and feel the love that begins to pour forth, you can take more steps and emerge as fully loving and compassionate individuals. Stripping away all that is unnecessary in your life may bring about fear at first, but gradually you will feel the freeing force of love springing up inside of you. In this stripping away from the grasp of demanding cultural norms comes not a mourning over your sacrifice, but a freedom from relinquishing superficial things which are no longer necessary for happiness.

This is clearly seen in an ancient story from *The Gospel of Thomas* by Jean-Yves Leloup of a gnostic who lived in utter simplicity although his family was wealthy and highly educated. A visitor came and asked the gnostic: "When did you decide to renounce riches and the world and why did you do it?"

"I never renounced the world," the gnostic replied. "I have never relinquished anything; it is the world that has renounced me. It is riches that have abandoned me—no doubt because I no longer needed them."

Once we have put aside the extraneous trappings of the world and return to simply being, we have space to hear the still, small voice within us that provides guidance, love, and support. Some people call it intuition, which means inner knowing. Some refer to this voice as their Higher Self. Others call it the Divine Presence within. This guidance is available to you 24/7, but you must be still and make space for receptivity.

Back to Basics

Getting back to basics opens up our compassionate nature, our natural state of being. In basic living, we find that we are no longer intoxicated with the illusion that busyness brings happiness. Quite the opposite is true. A complex life leads to more stress and strain, and lures us into forgetting our connection with God.

Here are some ways to simplify your life:

- Meditate daily. While this practice may seem to take up time, research shows that people who regularly practice

Transcendental Meditation (TM), for example, are more productive; they get more done in less time.

- Be still. Take a few minutes out of your day to practice mindful awareness. If you are in your office, look out the window and simply notice all that is around you whether it be grass, the sky, people, or cars moving by. You can also just listen and take in all the sounds around you. This will still your mind by absorbing the elements of the present moment. When your mind resides in the glory of stillness, you effortlessly bring peace and calm into the world of activity.
- Take an electronics fast. Put away the cell phone and turn off the computer, tablet, and television. Try this for one night a week and then expand it to several nights a week. See how your creativity and inner peace increase when electronic use decreases.
- Don't overschedule. Prioritize your day. See if there's anything that you can eliminate from your agenda to lighten your load. Don't overschedule your children. Let them have time to savor the wonder of childhood.
- Learn to say no. At a young age, we are taught that kindness means being polite, including saying yes to requests. Sometimes it is kinder to say no so that you are not acting from resentment or a sense of obligation.
- Create balance. Balance your life with work, play, rest, activity, and laughter. One way I incorporate laughter into my day is by having comedy sketches on my playlists;

when I'm at the gym or driving, a comedic sketch randomly comes on and I find myself laughing out loud wherever I am.

- Celebrate and value success in your life. I am not talking about success in the material world (although that will manifest with spiritual transformation), but success at forgiving, loving, being patient, not getting angry, noticing answered prayers, and seeing the grace in your life.
- Spend some time alone in the quietude of nature or listening to peaceful music. Take a brief walk, sit on a park bench, or go outside even for five minutes and breathe in the fresh air. Peaceful music will still the mind and the racing physiology.
- Fulfill your life's purpose. If your job is a struggle and a political war zone that leaves you depleted, think about shifting gears to something you are passionate about. Take small steps in that direction each week to bring that about. Believe in the power of God to work through you to create something new and wonderful.
- Spend some time each day in silence. Remove the earbuds, fast from social media, and stop watching YouTube for just a few moments and be silent. Listen to your inner voice and trust that whatever positive and nurturing guidance you receive is authentic. If you hear a critical or negative message that is not coming from your Higher Self but from the ego, it should be disregarded. Practice silence for yourself and those around you as well.

You don't always have to be talking to your spouse or family members. Taking some time for silence ensures that when you do speak it is meaningful, not mindless chatter.
- Give your gifts to the world. What are your gifts and talents? Are you giving them to the world? Why not answer your spiritual calling, which is your passion fueled by faith, and gift your gifts to the world? Nobody has your unique talents and abilities which were made to be enjoyed by the world. There is a power within you that knows what to do and how to do it, and you have vast resources that we cannot fathom with the human mind. Allow Spirit to work through you as a vehicle of expression and see how you come alive when doing your work. Trust that God works in glorious ways through you. Our work is meant to be a joyous expression of the Divine, a place where our passion comes alive.

Not for Mystics Only

Our minds are moving at breakneck speed. Technology, which is supposed to make life easier, keeps us glued to our phones, tablets, and computers. We feel we must be continually entertained and distracted, which prevents us from enjoying the simple pleasures in life. We are ruled by what the Buddhists call "monkey mind," which evokes images of screeching monkeys in our minds all demanding our attention. Our monkey minds are filled with excessive to-do lists, fear, anxiety, worry, panic, hurt, judgment, anger, and resentments. With all this going on in our minds, it is challenging to be mentally still, nurture our heart space, enjoy the present moment, and notice the beauty that surrounds us. As author Dorothy Salisbury Davis says, "Don't sell your soul to buy peanuts for the monkeys." There is a way to still this monkey mind and to directly experience the Divine Presence within, and that is through the simple and natural practice of meditation.

Meditation is one of the most essential practices for making space for compassion to grow. It steers the consciousness in the direction of spiritual growth and creates space for unbounded compassion. It is an ancient spiritual practice with a basis of unitive consciousness. It's also the foundation of health, peace, wisdom, joy, and love. Not only does meditation calm the busy mind, it also calms the physiology by releasing the outer stress that veils our connection with God. By stripping away the stress and quieting the mind, meditation puts you in deep communion with God. When the layers of stress are peeled away, there becomes space for bliss to emerge and for authentic kindness to grow.

Most people not practicing meditation are limited to their own identity and cannot expand to the Divine nature that exists in each one of us. If I ever miss a meditation (which is rare), I find myself saying, "I feel human today," because the bubbles of bliss disappear along with feeling the qualities of God within. Positive qualities are always there, but without meditation it is difficult to experience them; worse, there is a false feeling of separation from Source. Meditation is about accessing the God within. It allows you to feel the Divine Presence without trying or striving to do so. God moves from a concept to a direct experience. Regular meditation brings about a knowing that life is not about humanity; rather, it is about something much bigger than that. It is much like a rebirth from being human to experiencing who you are—an aspect of the one God who lives, breathes, and has its being in you. Only you can experience the transcendent for yourself—no one can do this for you. Spirit awaits your recognition of itself. Meditation is the way to recognize Spirit and invite it to express through you in all its majesty.

In the past, meditation had mystical connotations. Yet it is not for mystics, yogis, and monks alone. In fact, a recent Newsweek poll showed that nearly one-third of Americans meditate today. Dr. Woodson Merrell, executive director of Beth Israel Medical Center's planned Center for Health and Healing, describes meditation as "perhaps the most powerful tool for health."

Amid our busy lives, we have a way to calm down with a simple and natural practice. Meditation hushes the chatter in our minds, allowing us to listen to the voice of Spirit and feel the unbounded bliss of our true nature. Meditation is not contemplation and it is different from prayer; it is the direct experience of God. We don't meditate for the effects of what happens during the practice, but for the changes in ourselves in terms of opening our hearts. Answers may come in these sacred moments, although we are not asking for anything.

We should take time out daily to enter the silence and practice the simple art of meditation. During meditation, we feel less of our physical bodies and more of our true invisible life force. We move from the relative world of experience to experience the absolute. The purpose of meditation is not merely to experience this unbounded awareness while we are meditating, but to carry it through into activity so we directly experience our Source while we are at work, at home, in the grocery store, at a soccer game, or wherever we may be going about our daily activities. After meditation, we simply come back into activity refreshed, renewed, and with a deeper connection with God.

It's much like what Matthew spoke of in The Parable of the Hidden Treasure (13.44), "The kingdom of heaven is like a buyer looking for fine pearls. When he finds one that is unusually fine, he goes and sells everything that he has, and buys the pearl." Although it may appear to be buried, the pearl, or treasure, is already present in all its splendor and available to each one of us. With this in mind, we can approach meditation without strain, knowing that we are simply unearthing the precious jewel that is already present within us—a jewel that reveals all our beauty, bliss, and compassion. The practice goes beyond intellectual contemplation about spiritual matters to the direct experience of knowing God. Feeling something greater than ourselves, we gain firsthand experience of our connection with God, not only during the time of actual meditation but throughout the day. When you meditate, you will enjoy *satsanga*, which is a Sanskrit word that means "fellowship with God" ("sat" means "true" and "sanga" means "company").

When you meditate regularly, your true nature is experienced as that pure, vast expanse of bliss that is always within us but is often obscured by the stress, demands, fears, and worries of daily life. Meditation allows us to shed those stressors and feel our unity with all of life including God, humans, and animals. As we practice meditation, the energy of Divine Love is released through our thoughts, actions and speech, and pours out to the world as inspiration, compassion, and love. Simply stated, meditation is the key to accessing the kingdom of heaven on Earth.

Parmahansa Yogananda explains meditation in this beautiful way: "The greatest love you can experience is in communion with God in meditation. The love between the soul and Spirit is the perfect love, the love you are all seeking. When you meditate, love grows. Millions of thrills pass through your heart.... If you meditate deeply, a love will come over you such as no human tongue can describe; you will know His Divine love, and you will be able to give that pure love to others."

An ancient Sufi story tells us of a time when a man visited the Sufi master Nuri. He saw Nuri sitting in meditation, very still and without as much as a hair moving. He asked Nuri, "From where did you learn such deep meditation?"

Nuri said, "I learned from a cat waiting by a mouse hole. The cat was much stiller than I."

Most faith traditions encourage meditation practices. The Jewish people have Hitbonenut; Buddhists have *Zazen*, mindfulness, *metta*, *tonglen* (which is the Buddhist practice of sending and taking), and chanting of the Buddha's name. In the

Hindu tradition, there is Kriya Yoga and TM; the Sufis have a meditation practice that empties the mind to make space to become a ward of the Beloved. People from any faith tradition can meditate. There is an entire smorgasbord of meditation techniques to choose from. Some require that you repeat a mantra, which is a sound, syllable, or phrase that you repeat silently or out loud depending on the particular practice. Usually a qualified teacher gives you a mantra, which some believe is infused with Divine power. Other practices are based on a vocal chanting sound, breathing techniques, or focusing on an object. Some people like to focus on a passage from scripture or some other sacred writing.

No matter what meditation practice you choose, the direct experience of God is available to anyone regardless of faith, economic status, ethnicity, or gender. Yoganada tells us: "The surest sign that God exists is the increasing heart-bursting with joy felt in meditation… when you become increasingly intoxicated with the joy of meditation, and in making others happy by bestowing on them your divine peace—then you will know that God is with you always and that you are in Him."

Harvard researchers at Massachusetts General Hospital (MGH) have proven Yogananda's sentiments. The researchers found that meditation actually rebuilds the brain's grey matter in just eight weeks. According to Sara Lazar, a researcher with MGH's Psychiatric Neuroimaging Research Program and a Harvard Medical School instructor in psychology, while the practice of meditation is associated with a sense of peacefulness and physical relaxation, practitioners have long claimed that meditation also provides cognitive and psychological benefits that persist throughout the day. This study demonstrates that changes in the brain structure may underlie some of these reported improvements and that people are not just feeling better because they are spending more time relaxing.

Today, numerous studies prove the benefits of meditation and show how this practice can change the brain in ways that foster greater care and compassion for others. For example, when people who were adept in the practice of meditation watched videos of other people suffering, functional magnetic resonance image (fMRI) scans of their brains showed heightened activity mainly in structures that are important to care, nurturing, and positive social affiliations (in other words, the brain areas that orient them toward the well-being of others). By contrast, in non-meditators, the videos of suffering were more likely to engage brain structures that support unpleasant feelings such as sadness, aversion or pain. These feelings are what make people uncomfortable and want to flee from the situation. However, when the nonmeditators received meditation instruction—in this instance, the instruction was in the Buddhist method of lovingkindness—researchers saw shifts in brain activity including relatively less activation in neural structures that support uncomfortable feelings and thinking about oneself. When the new meditators viewed the videos after as little as one week of training, the researchers saw changes in brain response that suggest an intentional shift toward greater concern for the victim. The bottom line? If we train people in meditation, we may be able to shift neural responses in a direction that is more strongly oriented to caring for the well-being of others. Lovingkindness and compassion spring from the simple and natural practice of meditation.

The best practice for you is one that resonates with you and has been scientifically proven to change brain waves in a positive way. For this, it is best to learn from a qualified teacher. While I give guidelines for meditation in this section that you can follow, it's a good idea to engage with a teacher who specializes in meditation and who can give you specific instruction to guide you on your path. Meditation must be incorporated into your own life as regularly as brushing your teeth so it can do its natural work of transforming your awareness. One of my meditation teachers said that meditating is like eating chocolate cake: it's not a sacrifice but something that you want to do.

Most meditation teachers agree that 20 minutes twice a day (once in the morning before your day begins and again before dinner after a hectic day of activity) is called for in order for a shift in consciousness to take place. Try to meditate at the same time each day so it becomes part of your daily routine. If this is not possible for you, then any amount of time will do—whatever fits into your schedule best. Just take the first step and begin to practice. You likely spend lots of time online, watching TV, running around to activities and meeting the demands of everyday life, so why not take a few minutes more out of each day for an activity that promotes deep transformation and brings peace, bliss, and joy to you and those whose lives you touch? For now, just schedule it in for yourself even if you don't have 20 minutes twice a day. Do what you can. And remember not to have a preconceived agenda when you sit down to practice—just allow the experience to be what it is.

People sometimes judge their practice as good or bad, deep or shallow, but whatever occurs during practice, trust that important changes are going on underneath the surface. For example, if you have a lot of thoughts that intrude on your practice, it could be that those thoughts are coming up for healing or for stress release. When needed, actively remember that your efforts are never wasted. As Sri Krishna tells us in the *Bhagavad Gita*, "On this path, effort never goes to waste, and there is no failure. Even a little effort toward spiritual awareness will protect you from the greatest fear."

Below is a brief look at some meditation practices to give you a feel for the variety of techniques available. Remember, it's best to learn to meditate from a qualified teacher who is proficient in the technique he or she practices.

Mother Meditation

One beautiful technique is described by the Dalai Lama in his book, *Essence of the Heart Sutra*. It is often known as the Mother Meditation. He tells us to "visualize every being as your own beloved mother or as another person for whom you have the utmost affection—someone who for you embodies great kindness." He tells us to "call up the feelings of affection that arise with regard to one's mother or another maternally kind and loving person and then extend those feelings to every other being, perceiving that each being has been equally kind and loving to you." He says the visualization of maternal lovingkindness helps us to realize our interconnectedness with others and to generate lovingkindness to all. In the words of the Buddha, "Love the whole world as a mother loves her only child."

Centering Prayer

Centering prayer is a meditation technique in the Christian tradition founded by Father Thomas Keating. This heart-centered method is a practice of letting go of thoughts and simply being available to God. Unlike other practices that focus on attention matters, centering prayer is based on your intention to experience God. As with all meditation practices, we let go of thinking what the outcome should be and surrender to whatever comes about during the practice. Father Keating describes it this way: centering prayer is not so much the absence of thoughts as detachment from them. It is the opening of mind and heart, body and emotions—our whole being—to God, the Ultimate Mystery, beyond words, thoughts, and emotions—beyond, in other words, the psychological content of the present moment. In centering prayer, we do not deny or repress what is in our conscious thinking process. We simply accept the fact of whatever is there and go beyond it, not by effort but by letting go of whatever is there.

The first step in this practice is to choose a short word or phrase that you resonate with. It could be Holy Spirit, Divine Love, Jesus, Dear Lord, or Open Heart, for example. You can choose any one- or two-syllable word combination that sets your intention in motion.

The phrase is a symbol of your intention to experience God's presence within. As with most meditation practices, it's best to do this practice sitting up with legs uncrossed and your head erect.

Gently close your eyes. You can begin with a short prayer if you like. Take a few long, deep breaths and begin to silently say your sacred word. At some point your sacred word will fall away from your consciousness and you will stop thinking. Once thoughts arise again, say your sacred word to release the thought and bring yourself back to stillness. Just continue with this pattern of letting go of thinking and then bringing your mind back to the sacred word when thoughts crop up. It is recommended that you practice centering prayer for 20 minutes twice a day. When you are finished practicing, take a few moments to rest with your eyes closed and gently come back into activity.

Lovingkindness Meditation

In the Buddhist tradition, it's called *metta*. Quite simply, this means lovingkindness as well as friendliness, benevolence and nonviolence. The Pali word "metta" has two meanings. One is the word for "gentle," while the other root meaning is "friend." Think of a relationship as a chance to practice metta—to be a good friend to yourself and others. A friend loves us unconditionally and offers encouragement and support to us when we need it. A friend offers a soft place to land when we are frightened or face hurdles in our lives.

Much like a caterpillar in a tight chrysalis that breaks open when the conditions are right, the sweet practice of metta cracks open the heart to its full capacity to love. Metta yields unbounded joy and a deeper connection with the one heart, one life, and one love, which is God. The practice of metta, or lovingkindness meditation, helps us become a good friend to ourselves and others by releasing negative energy. All negative emotions can be met with lovingkindness, shifting our essence from tumultuous to peaceful. Metta helps us to awaken the love that resides in our hearts that already exists no matter how badly someone hurts us. This lovingkindness meditation helps us let go of resentments, grudges, and bitterness. Through practice, we are opened to offer love to people we already love and to those we are feeling hatred or anger towards. This meditation is a powerful tool for forgiving. Since we don't have any self-interest when practicing this method, we create the foundation of unconditionally loving relationships. Through offering genuine love, we effortlessly release hate, anger, bitterness, greed, and selfishness from our minds. In short, the practice frees us and gives us space to become more compassionate and loving. This ancient practice that the Buddha taught creates magnificent love and tenderness in both the one practicing the meditation and the one on the receiving end. By shifting our consciousness and infusing our hearts with lovingkindness, we rise to a higher vibration. We develop a deeper connection with the Divine.

Basically, what you are doing when practicing the lovingkindness meditation is awakening the lovingkindness within us and then offering it to yourself, someone you love, a stranger, an enemy and, ultimately, to all beings on Earth. Many Buddhist masters teach metta and I suggest that you find one to teach you if you are interested in this practice. In the meantime, here is a brief look at how it works.

To begin, sit comfortably on a chair or on a meditation cushion, keeping your spine straight, and close your eyes. Take some deep breaths. Relax your physical body and focus on your breathing. Shift the focus on your breath to your heart as you begin the practice. And again, breathe normally. Now gently recite phrases of good for yourself first, then for loved ones and then for those who have caused you pain or distress.

Repeat phrases for yourself such as:

> *May I be happy.*
> *May I be peaceful.*
> *May I be healthy.*
> *May I be loved.*

If you prefer, you may replace these phrases with ones that have more meaning for you—for example, I sometimes add, "May I feel the Divine Presence within." Just be sure to keep the phrases simple, from the heart and to the point.

Next, choose someone to offer metta to. For this section of the practice, choose to send lovingkindness to someone you love. Select someone who makes your heart overflow with love when you think of that person. Examples of a loved one who elicits such deep feelings of love might be your child, mother, father, or a friend. When you decide on who to send love to, picture your loved one's face in your mind as you begin the phrases.

Repeat phrases for your loved one such as:

> *May you be happy.*
> *May you be peaceful.*
> *May you be healthy.*
> *May you be loved.*

Spend as much time as you like reciting the phrases and when you feel a sense of being done, move on to the third phase.

You are going to offer lovingkindness to a stranger, sometimes known in Buddhism as "the neutral person." This might be someone who you see on the bus each morning, someone who you buy coffee from at the café, or someone who helps you at the pet store, for example.

Bring this person's image to mind and begin repeating the phrases:

> *May you be happy.*
> *May you be peaceful.*
> *May you be healthy.*
> *May you be loved.*

This is when things get tricky. You will next send lovingkindness to someone who is referred to as "the enemy." This person could be a family member, a colleague, a friend, or, perhaps, a love interest who has hurt you, harmed you, disappointed you, or angered you in some way. The person could be someone in your present life or someone from long ago (even someone who has passed on). Remember that when you offer lovingkindness to someone who hurt you, you are not condoning actions or saying that they were right. You may not even have an understanding of why the situation unfolded as it did. In any and every case, the power of love diffuses all negative emotions. You will feel the energy shift as you move forward in this segment of the meditation practice.

Begin sending kindness to this person by saying:

> *May you be happy.*
> *May you be peaceful.*
> *May you be healthy.*
> *May you be loved.*

As you practice, keep in mind that this person who seems like a monster in your mind has the same desire for health, happiness, peace, and love as you do. You may struggle with offering lovingkindness to someone who has hurt you. Be tender with yourself and don't judge. Instead, gently bring your mind to that person and picture him or her in your mind's eye. Feel this person's presence. Think about love extending out from you and from God, caressing that person who is receiving this love and kindness. Picture lovingkindness flowing through them. As you repeat these phrases, you will feel a shift in energy and a deep abiding peace encapsulating your heart.

Be sure to spend as much time offering lovingkindness to your seeming enemy as for those you love. Sit with the deep sense of peace in your heart space. Once you finish the practice, simply sit and quietly offer lovingkindness to other people or the Earth, animals and sea life. Return to the present moment by gently opening your eyes, and bring the energy of this peace and love along with your strengthened conviction that everyone is inherently good into your day and to everyone you meet.

Kriya Yoga

Kriya Yoga is a type of meditation that focuses on the breath. In Sanskrit, "kri" means "kara dhatu"—action of the elements—and "a" means "soul" or "atma." The first and most important action of the soul is breath. The word "yoga" comes from the Sanskrit word "Yuj," which means "union"—the union of the individual soul with Spirit. Kriya Yoga is a way to attain the union of the breath and soul in each inhalation and exhalation. In other words, the union of the individual soul with Spirit is called Kriya Yoga.

Kriya Yoga is an ancient yoga system that has been revived in modern times by Mahavatar Babaji through his disciple Lairi Mahasaya. It was made popular in the West by Paramahansa Yogananda. Yogananda says that Kriya Yoga gives the true experience of spirituality as follows:

"Your life will reflect spiritual consciousness if you meditate. Since the publication of my book [*Autobiography of a Yogi*], everyone is asking about Kriya Yoga. That is my purpose. I didn't come to give theological abstractions, but a technique whereby those who are sincere can truly know God, not just theorize about Him... the practice of Kriya gives the true experience of religion, which cannot be had by just talking about God. Jesus said, 'Why call ye me, Lord, Lord, and not do the things which I say?'"

Kriya Yoga is said to bring deep peace, bliss, and joy. The technique consists of a number of levels of pranayama (breath) methods that are designed to hasten spiritual advancement through communion with God.

In fact, the sacred Hindu text, the *Bhagavad Gita*, refers to Kriya Yoga and states, "Offering inhaling breath into the outgoing breath, and offering the outgoing breath into the inhaling breath, the yogi neutralizes both these breaths; he [or she] thus releases the life force from the heart and brings it under his [or her] control."

In the book *Journey to Self-Realization,* Yogananda states: "When by Kriya Yoga I open my spiritual eye, the whole world drops away from my consciousness, and God is with me. And why not? I am his child. St. Ignatius said, 'God seeks willing hearts that He may give his bounties to them....' That is most beautiful, and that is what I believe. God seeks willing hearts for the bestowal of his gifts. He is willing to give us everything, but we are not willing to make the effort to be receptive."

Pure Land Buddhist Meditation

Pure Land Buddhism is widely practiced in Asia. In this chanting meditation, we are asking Amitabha Buddha to help us gain enlightenment and help us be born in the Pure Land. Buddhists believe this is where there are beings who advance along the Buddhist path and never again fall back into samsara. Samsara is the endless cycle of suffering caused by birth, death, and rebirth.

According to Pure Land Buddhists, we will be able to continue our practice in the Pure Land or when we choose to return to this and other worlds to help others. We do so without being affected by unfavorable environments or our former bad habits. If we wish, we will all be able to do this even before we attain enlightenment.

The benefits of this easy practice are that:

- It is easy and can be done almost anywhere
- There is no difficult entry criterion
- Due to the vows of Amitabha Buddha (who vowed to help those who call his name), achievement can be attained more quickly and easily than with other practices

We simply chant, "Amituofo," which is the name of Amitabha Buddha in Chinese. As we chant and the mind focuses on the sound of Amituofo, errant thoughts are replaced with pure thoughts as we create less negative karma. After Amitabha has been in our mind continuously for a long time, our true nature—our Buddha nature—will be uncovered. When we chant with the sole thought of Amituofo, we form a connection with him—and become one with him. In that instance, we are in the Pure Land—far to the west and deep within.

If you are interested in learning more about Pure Land Buddhism, visit their web site listed in the Resources section of this book.

Transcendental Meditation (TM)

The TM practice is based on the ancient Vedic tradition of enlightenment in India. This sacred wisdom has been handed down by Vedic masters from generation to generation for thousands of years. About fifty years ago, Maharishi Mehesh Yogi—the representative in our age of Vedic tradition—introduced TM to the world, restoring the knowledge and experience of higher states of consciousness at a critical time for humanity. When TM is taught today, the teachers maintain the same procedures used by the teachers of thousands of years ago for maximum effectiveness. Author Alice Walker said: "At one point I learned Transcendental Meditation. This was thirty-something years ago. It took me back to the way that I naturally was as a child growing up way in the country, rarely seeing people. I was in that state of oneness with creation and it was as if I didn't exist except as part of everything."

TM is a simple, natural, effortless technique practiced by more than 5 million people worldwide today. People of all ages, cultures, and religions practice this simple, natural method. Generally, one practices it for 20 minutes twice a day white sitting comfortably with closed eyes. It's not a religion, philosophy, or lifestyle. It is, however, the most widely practiced, most researched, and most effective method of meditation in the world today. To learn this technique, you need a qualified teacher of TM.

In brief, the TM technique allows your mind to settle inwardly beyond thought to experience the source of thought—pure awareness, also known as transcendental consciousness. This is the most silent and peaceful level of consciousness—your innermost self. In this state of restful alertness, your brain functions with significantly greater coherence and your body achieves deep rest.

For more information on the TM technique, visit their web site listed in the Resources section of this book.

Bliss Revealed

With the slightest of effort to be receptive by practicing meditation, we can deepen our realization of God and live in the highest states of consciousness where bliss, peace, love and joy are revealed as our natural states of being. Just remember that whatever practice you adopt, no meditation time is ever wasted, even if the mind wanders. As Saint Francis de Sale advises: "If the heart wanders or is distracted, bring it back to the point quite gently and replace it tenderly in its Master's presence. And even if you did nothing during the whole of your hour but bring your heart back and place it again in our Lord's presence, though it went away every time you brought it back, your hour will be very well employed."

Kindness in Action

When Carol stopped at Kentucky Fried Chicken (KFC) to buy lunch, she felt a strong urge to pay for whatever a man and his family who were behind her in line would order. Her friends grumbled and pointed out that those people had a brand-new vehicle and Carol didn't need to pay for them. Ignoring her friends' grumblings, Carol said, "I don't care about that; I still need to do it." She paid for the family's meal anyway, and it was a large sum of money. Carol said she "felt right about it" so she parked over to the side to wait for her food to get ready.

The man she treated approached her car and he was crying. He said, "I don't know how to thank you because my wife is at home and she is about to pass away." He told Carol that he wanted to take the kids out and they were hungry so he brought them to KFC. He was flat broke and had sold his home, his possessions, and even this vehicle to pay for his wife's medical expenses. Carol felt it was Divine Mind that had directed her to pay for this particular family's meal. Moved further, Carol and her friends contributed more money to this man and his family so they could buy food for the next day as well.

Carol tells us that she listens to her intuition to do things that are good. "You have an overwhelming feeling of love and that comes over your whole body, knowing that it's divine love, saying you need to help these people." She added, "You need to give whether someone looks rich or poor. It doesn't matter what they look like; if you get the urge to give, pay attention to it. You don't look at what you see on the outside, you look at what's inside your heart and it's universal law saying, 'Come on.' Let universal love take control of you and put its presence in you for everyone to see."

Affirmation

In loving communion with God I find bliss beyond compare and realization of my true nature.

Chapter Ten

Empty the Trash

"Fulfill my joy by being like-minded, having the same love, being of one accord, of one mind. Let nothing be done through selfish ambition or conceit, but in lowliness of mind let each esteem others better than himself. Let each of you look out not only for his own interests, but also for the interests of others."
— PHILIPPIANS 2:2–2:4

We are living in a society that is plagued with materialism, consumerism, greed, corruption, and competition. We get filled up with negative emotions and bombarded with false messages that say we need certain things to be happy. Many of our corporations and leaders have disregard for the environment. Our beloved wildlife animals are suffering from human activities aimed at them such as: brutal aerial wolf hunts, pesticide use that destroys Monarch butterfly habitats, shark finning—an inhumane practice in which shark fins are hacked off, leaving the sharks unable to swim, and organic pollution that threatens polar bears and their food sources.

The ego's creations such as anger, greed, fear, and clinging is the trash that takes up space in our hearts, minds, and souls. With our culture's pull for us to fill up with what we don't need, there is not much room for love and compassion, let alone God's divinity within us, to be experienced in totality. Our dualistic minds trick us into thinking that this is the normal way of humanity. Thankfully, we can effectively alleviate human-made problems by embracing the spiritual way. How, exactly, can we remedy these negative human creations? We need to make room for God by emptying ourselves of toxic thoughts and emotions and putting on the mind of Christ—a practice used not only in Christianity but in other faith traditions as well. For example, the Sufis practice self-emptying through meditation that empties the mind to open a space for the Beloved Presence. The concept of emptiness, called *shunyata*, is also practiced by Buddhists. It is explained in depth in the book the *Heart Sutra* by the Dalai Lama. The Jewish tradition includes the practice Hitbodedut, which is a form of meditation taught by Rebbe Nachman of Breslove. This is a process of emptying in order to refill with vision and spirit. The Hitbodedut meditation frees one of negativity that obstructs spiritually, transforming nondual realization and divinity of all.

The Christians look to ascended master Jesus Christ as a great example of self-emptying, which is what we are going to explore in this chapter. No matter what your faith tradition, self-emptying is an important practice universal to all. With the practice of self-emptying in Christianity, Jesus showed us a way of living which, in short, means breaking free of clinging, losing all notions of the "I," and relying on the Divine Presence for everything. He shows us the need to move away from the egocentric dualistic operating system which thrives on separateness into unitive consciousness that can be gleaned only from deep within the heart space. Jesus's self-emptying is an example of how he did not cling to his divinity. Rather, he descended to Earth to join the human race and minister to people by relying on the Holy Spirit. Jesus descended into form and was willing to empty himself to become human. Jesus was divine and human at the same time. In much the same way, the Divine Presence eternally lives within us. All we need to do is allow our humanness to fade away, and rely on Divine Principle for everything. It's not that we become empty to be filled with the Divine Presence, because we already are filled with it; rather, we become empty to reveal the Divine light of God that is eternally present but all too often covered up by the ego's creations.

The Beauty of Kenosis

This lovely and vitally important practice is formally called *kenosis*, a Greek word meaning "letting go" or "emptying oneself." Emptying is a nonclinging—a willingness to let everything be taken away and still be happy. This practice is beautifully outlined in St. Paul's letter to the Philippians, an early Christian hymn that describes what it means to put on the mind of Christ. Some say Paul wrote this hymn when he was jailed and even may have been chained at the time. It's also known as the Epistle of Joy.

The following excerpt from Philippians 2:9–16 of the hymn is taken from a translation by the monks of New Camaldoli Hermitage, Big Sur, California. The monks kindly sent me their version of St. Paul's beautiful hymn from their hymnal to share with you here. This hymn demonstrates what Christians believe putting on the mind of Christ means.

> *"Though his state was that of God,*
> *Yet he did not deem equality with God*
> *something that he should cling to.*
>
> *Rather, he emptied himself,*
> *and assuming the state of a slave,*
> *he was born in human likeness.*
>
> *He, being known as one of us,*
> *Humbled himself, obedient unto death,*
> *even death on a cross.*
>
> *For this, God raised him on high*
> *and bestowed on him the name*
> *which is above every other name.*
>
> *So that, at the name of Jesus,*
> *every knee should bend*
> *in heaven, and on earth and under the earth.*
>
> *And so every tongue should proclaim*
> *'Jesus Christ is Lord!'*
> *To God the Father's glory."*

In this verse, Paul recognizes that by emptying himself, Jesus descended into human form. By dying on the cross, he emptied himself even further as he fell downward, only to rise up in glory. Throughout all of Jesus' life and no matter what situation he faced, he continued with the practice of self-emptying. This may seem like a spiritual contradiction since many of us were taught from a young age that everything having to do with God is upward whether it's our idea of heaven, angels, or Jacob dreaming of the ladder going up toward heaven. From Paul's hymn, we learn that, contrary to our traditional beliefs about ascension, we grow in unitive consciousness by self-emptying, not by going up but by going down by, for example, humbling ourselves. Jesus reached the lowest point but then was exalted by God. His crucifixion was a humiliating and shameful way to die. Despite this, Jesus modeled the path of kenosis that we can, and should, use in our everyday lives. Keep in mind that kenosis is not a theory; it is a practice as important as prayer, meditation, and silence.

The descent of Spirit into form is not exclusive to Christianity. It is taught in other faith traditions as well. For example, in metaphysical teachings, such as the Science of Mind, there is a descent of Spirit into form much like the Divine descending into human form. Dr. Ernest Holmes, founder of Religious Science, teaches that Spirit descends into form first into "universal soul" or "universal subjectivity," which operates on thought and descends further into form. Holmes tells us: "It is necessary that Spirit be manifested in order to express Itself.... Man reenacts the whole Universal Life, and his nature is identical with Spirit. What is true of the Whole is true of any one of its undivided parts. Man comes to a point of individualization in the Whole and is subject to the Law of the Whole."

Jesus also modeled humility as a virtue in contrast to living in a self-absorbed fashion. No matter what your faith tradition is, it's a good idea to grow compassion by modeling humility, putting others' welfare first and living for the well-being of others (much like the Buddhist bodhisattva). Whatever circumstance Jesus was in, he reacted by self-emptying. Although Jesus was in the form of the Divine, he exercised great humility by emptying himself and becoming like us to the extreme humiliation of dying on the cross. Taking this path is the key to human transformation and awakening.

This hymn inspires us to take on the mind of Christ, which is to have the same mind that Jesus used, which is the mind of God. In metaphysical teachings, it is believed that there is only one Mind, this Mind is our mind, and it operates in, as, and through us. We don't have to go anywhere to access a God out there somewhere because God is within us right now. There is no mythical manlike form with a long white beard and wielding a staff. Rather, God is a perfect indwelling presence and power within each one of us. Dr. Ernest Holmes tells us, "We have the mind of Christ in such a degree as we trust implicitly in the universe, and no longer do things which contradict the fundamental goodness.... Every man has the mind of Christ... but can only use this Mind when is in harmony with Life."

Making Room for God

In our stressful and demanding world where we are continually filled up with regrets, sorrow, suffering, anxiety, unresolved relationships, anger, hostility, violence, and busyness, how, exactly, is it possible to self-empty and make space for God's action in us? First, we must become self-aware and discover what undesirable traits we are filled with. Take a moment to sit in silence and ask yourself these questions: Do you have fear? Anger? Greed? Selfishness? Pettiness? Negativity? Ask yourself what you need to rid yourself of to put on the mind of Christ. Can you let go of the false self, or small self, to make room for the true self of our Divine nature? Consider that Jesus was both human and divine. Can you see that you have those qualities within you as well?

Self-emptying is accomplished when we live totally dependent on Divine Principle for everything in our lives. We trust our Source for everything that we need, which breeds generosity, love, compassion and kindness. We are living from deep immersion in God's presence when our hearts are overflowing with gratitude, when we are fully open and receptive to being an instrument of the Divine and are coming from a heart space of love and compassion. Now the practice of self-emptying flows naturally and is not forced or a facade; rather, it is a natural result of responding to God's love. This means that we move our mindset away from the ways of the world and move toward compassion and caring for other beings—for all of creation including humans, animals, and the Earth. This entails transforming our thoughts away from anything unlike God, and depending on Divine Principle for everything in our lives.

Just like the Buddhist practice of nonclinging, Jesus' message is to let go of clinging, to let everything go and to be generous beyond measure. Jesus was generous with healing the sick, feeding the multitudes, and giving up his life as an example of ultimate love for humankind. Suffering and dying on the cross exemplifies not even clinging to life itself. When we can fully engage in life, we stop clinging to any of its forms. We can pour everything out of ourselves without regret, thus walking the path of self-emptying. The Buddhists and Christians agree on the concept of self-emptying. In fact, Dilgo Khyentse, author of *The Heart of Compassion: The Thirty-Seven Verses on the Practice of Bodhisattvas*, tells us: "A thorough, experiential understanding of emptiness is the only antidote to the belief in an 'I,' in a truly existing self. Once you recognize emptiness, all your attachment to such a self will vanish without a trace.... You will be free of self-cherishing, compassion will arise spontaneously, and you will benefit beings without any effort."

The practice of self-emptying is essential to growing authentic kindness. It is not seen in random acts of kindness which may be a good place to start but don't encompass the whole of the teaching. If we would all incorporate a bit of kenosis in our daily lives and move beyond focus on the self to focus on others, we would experience deep love and inner peace no matter what is going on around us. Society will function better with people who practice self-emptying. The key to peace on Earth is to let go of the focus on "I" and exemplify compassion and lovingkindness through self-emptying. To put on the mind of Christ is something everyone can do no matter what faith tradition you belong to. We can move away from the narrow mindset in our culture today and care for other beings and all of creation with love and compassion. Practicing kenosis is a spiritual strength because you are a warrior who is not buying into the cultural norms but has the courage to pave new ground with stones of compassion, love, gentleness, kindness and care for all of humanity. It is something our world cries out for and we can create a space for love, freedom, wholeness, and humility. It is a way of peace, stillness, and joy.

Giving compassion is one way to practice self-emptying. Doing so ignites the light of God within us, raising our vibration so that we touch the lives of humans and every living thing on our planet in a positive way, and it extends out to touch the lives of others. When we are empty of negative traits, we are agents of love and compassion to all living things. As shepherds of a new age of kindness, we can change conditions of suffering and let the Christ light shine from within us to heal, to love, and to effect change. This is precisely what is meant by "putting on the mind of Christ." It means to be empty of anything unlike God to the extent that we give up attachment to our humanity, to the ridiculous grasp of the world of form, and let our true spirituality emerge. When we are empty of the unnecessary grab of the world of form, only then do we fully experience our Divine Nature. False attachments prevent us from experiencing the full nature of the Divine within. When we are empty, there is a space created and God rushes in to fill it with love, kindness, compassion and peace. This is accomplished when you are empty and prepared to walk your sacred path.

This hymn unlocks the door to a compassionate world derived from making a space for God in your heart. To be able to do this, we must engage with this teaching and examine ourselves to see if we are truly putting on the mind of Christ in our heart and soul. Once we are doing so through self-emptying, the enlightening words of Paul can live in our hearts and give birth to a new awareness within us. We discover that the space within is the space that contains the Divinity that lies within each one of us. Only in this sacred space away from the lures of the material world can we be in deep connection with all that is good and all that is Divine.

As Meister Eckhart says, "When God finds you ready and empty, he must act and fill you to overflowing with himself, just as sunlight must flood and fill the clear, pure air. He cannot fail to do this when he finds you so empty and bare." Meister Eckhart is telling us to be naked and empty before God. One magnificent illustration of this point is from *Logion 37* from *The Gospel of Thomas*.[1]

> "His disciples asked:
>
> When will be the day that you appear to us?
>
> When will be the day of our vision?
>
> Yeshua replied:
>
> On the day when you are naked
>
> as newborn infants
>
> who trample their clothing,
>
> then you will see the Son of the Living One
>
> and you will have no more fear."

Authentic Kindness

This gospel encourages us to be bare before God, to shed all our Earthly pulls and fascinations, to be without negativity and without the ego, without clinginess, hate, greed or selfishness. We must let all of it go so that we can see and feel the Divine Presence that fills us up when we are stripped bare of the attractions of the world. It takes trust to rely solely on Divine Principle and to shed the attachment to the world of form. But when we do strip ourselves bare and trust in Divine Principle for everything, we find a love bursting in our hearts that is unstoppable, and compassion becomes our only way of being in the world. It's an ecstatic place to live, in the sacredness of the most high. This doesn't mean we are outcasts from the world, sequestered in a cave somewhere. Not at all. It means that we bring our inner light to every situation and are fully equipped with a heart brimming with unconditional and compassion to administer kindness in this world of form and while maintaining our attachment be to the Divine Presence from which all good stems.

This beautiful poem by Jacques Laccarrière illustrates what it means to self-empty and be naked before God.

"Unlearning. Deconditioning your birth.
Forgetting your name. Going naked.

Sloughing away your last remains. Disrobing your memory.
Melting down your masks.

Ripping up your duties. Dismantling your certainties.
Disconnecting your doubts. Losing control of your being.

Barbara Gulbranson

Unbaptizing your springs. Unmapping your roads.
Shearing your desires. Gutting your passions.

Desacralizing the prophets. Discrediting the future.
Overturning the past. Discouraging Time.

Unknotting unreason. Deflowering delirium.
Defrocking the sacred. Sobering up from vertigo.

Defacing Narcissus. Delivering Gilead.
Deposing Moloch. Dethroning Leviathan.

Demystifying blood. Dissecting the monkey.
Disinheriting the ancestor.

Unburdening your soul. Unfailing your failures.
Disenchanting your despair. Unchaining your hope.

Delivering your madness. Defusing your fears.
Disencumbering your heart. Disappointing your Death.

Debasing your basis. Shredding your acquistions.
Unlearn. Become naked."

Kindness in Action

In her book, *Cancer: What to Do or Say,* the now deceased Claudia Mulcahy relates how kindness helped heal her soul during her cancer experience. She explained how, during the week of her diagnosis of cancer, four complete strangers complimented her without knowing what was going on in her world. They talked about things she couldn't lose from cancer. "What a great sense of color and style you have." "You have the most beautiful eyes." "You can get anything with that smile. Anything. What a beautiful smile." This comment was from a guy at Can and Bottle Recycle who let her go ahead of him in line. Claudia said, "His compliment about my smile was just what I needed to hear—then I began to cry." When she began to cry, the man exclaimed, "What? Did you pay your taxes yesterday?"

Claudia was so surprised that she shared her news with him. She said he had "genuine compassion and gave me a gentle, but sincere hug." He told her that he was working at the Catholic elementary school across the street and offered to say a prayer for her. "God bless you," the man said.

Claudia responded, "God does bless me. I'm a bit pissed off right now—but God does bless me." The man grinned and nodded, "What you are feeling is normal. Be okay with that."

The following week, Claudia had enough energy to bake some lemon bars and she took them to the school office.

"This is going to sound really strange," she told the office personnel. They replied, "We've heard it all."

Claudia explained how she met a man who worked there and the office workers said that he was Bob, the PE coach. They looked all over for him but he was gone. So Claudia left the lemon bars, feeling comfort that an angel worked just a block away from her apartment.

Claudia explained, "The universe supports us. If we are open, we'll see the support everywhere. Spirit worked through these people, letting me know I wouldn't walk alone. We never know what's going on in the lives of those around us. My experiences from these encounters with strangers were reminders that Spirit works in, around, through, and for us."

Affirmation

Life is a precious gift. I live each day to the fullest spreading love, light, and compassion wherever I go.

Chapter Eleven

Awaken to Your World of Transformation

"Metamorphosis has always been the greatest symbol of change for poets and artists. Imagine that you could be a caterpillar one moment and a butterfly the next."
— LOUIE SCHWARTZBERG

As we take these teachings into our hearts, we will see transformation in our individual lives and in the lives we touch. The only place to begin world reform is within ourselves. If we shower everything with lovingkindness with the intention to alleviate suffering in others, we are taking major steps in our own realization and awakening. We can use this precious life to open our hearts and minds to a greater state of livingness—one that reveres the unity of all beings on Earth. We can step out of our comfort zone and embrace a new way of living.

Our minds are much like baby elephants in captivity. The elephants are chained for a few short months and begin to believe they can never be free. Even after the chain is removed, the elephants do not leave. They never wander beyond the constraints of the small area of their former captivity. Like the elephants, we forget that we have the freedom to expand our horizons beyond the dictates of the material world and beyond our comfort zone. We must realize that if we are to experience more of life, we must move beyond the human constraints of our minds even if it's only by one baby step at a time. We have to courageously step out where our hearts have never ventured before and begin walking a new and sacred path. These teachings empower us to do so by saturating us with love and compassion to offer to others. We now live in a state where authentic kindness is revealed in everything we say, do, and touch. Whether we are angry, sad, hurting or even happy, that becomes a vehicle through which we can offer authentic kindness at that very moment. We are then able to experience the infinite bliss of giving kindness to ourselves and others, which is our natural state of being.

Even the smallest seeds of kindness can reap the greatest harvest. A smile, a light touch, and a helping hand can be instrumental in growing vast fields of love. Indeed, love is the driving force behind all outpourings of kindness. For without love how could we have compassion, forgiveness, generosity, or unitive consciousness? This love, which is the living presence of Spirit, empowers you to bestow kindness on yourself and others not for personal gain or accolades, but for the sheer thrill of alleviating someone else's pain for a moment or for a lifetime.

God's light shines bright in the heart that is open and receptive to love, the heart that is basked in compassion, the heart that gives unceasingly and longs to alleviate the suffering in others. With love and compassion at the core of our being, we can use every circumstance, every trial and every tribulation as a step on the ladder of human transformation and awakening. You don't have to be a mystic or sage, everyone can do it. This beautiful and sacred way of life is needed in our demanding world today. This is the path of awakened beings. This is the path of the fearless. This is the path of love.

May you take these teachings into your heart for your own personal growth and for the benefit of others now and always.

Appendix One

Developing Bodhichitta Attitude

Getting a bodhichitta attitude, an attitude of lovingkindness, will transform not only your life but the lives of those you come in contact with. Basically, it will make the world a kinder, gentler, more loving place to live in. So how, then, do you develop an awakened heart-mind as you go about your daily life with its many demands and frustrations? All it takes is growth of consciousness and a desire to free others from suffering. Take a look at the checklist below to see if your consciousness is ready and willing.

1. *Do you live your life in service to others?* Being less focused on the self and more focused on helping others is a sure sign of bodhichitta attitude. This calling may require you to volunteer at an organization or simply give from your heart on a day-to-day basis.
2. *Are you fulfilling your life purpose?* This means refusing to be in a career that depletes you, is mundane, or is something you are doing just for income. It means knowing what your gifts are and stepping out into a field that you are passionate about even if you risk security. When you give your gifts to the world, you feel energized, kinder, and alive because Spirit is working in you, as you and through you.

3. *Do you feel the interconnectedness of all?* When you live in unitive consciousness, you simply can't stand to hurt another person or an animal because you intuitively experience the oneness of all. You feel a deep connection to other people and all of nature, and feel your heart steeped in love as you gaze upon all living beings.
4. *Are you engaged in a regular spiritual practice?* This may not be religious, though it is spiritual in nature. Spiritual practice can be as simple as being in silence, praying, meditating, walking in the woods, listening to music, or taking that much-needed rest from electronics to simply be.
5. *Do you practice generosity daily?* Giving abundantly is required to reach higher states of consciousness. It's a good idea to give something away every day and see how this expands your heart space. Just give without expecting anything in return and watch what happens.
6. *Can you accept that some people will betray, abandon, and hurt you, and can you accept this without becoming vengeful or bitter?* Deep wisdom is gained from every experience, and we can use any challenge as an impetus for greater growth and softening of the heart. We can also understand that nonattachment to form (form is always changing) is the foundation of higher states of awareness.
7. *If you become angry, can you use that emotion for growth and transformation?* Anger can teach you how to stay even-minded in times of discord. And remember, anger is not

destructive when it leads to effective world change by peaceful methods.

8. *Do you understand that your thinking outpictures as the conditions in your life?* Replace gripes and complaints with a positive and cheerful attitude to change your circumstances and become a bright light in the lives of others. You ARE a powerful cocreator with God.

9. *Do you love with all your heart and soul, giving love and never asking for, or seeking, anything in return?* Loving unconditionally is the true nature of bodhichitta attitude.

10. *Can you stop feeling badly about yourself and honor who you are, just the way you are?* Getting off the treadmill of unworthiness is essential for spiritual growth. You are made in the image and likeness of God, which means not that you look like God but that you have all the same qualities within you such as love, peace, beauty, abundance, power and wisdom. When you berate yourself, you berate God's perfect creation.

11. *Do you have fears that prevent you from fully engaging in life?* Fear can be a crippling hindrance or it can be an agent of great change in your life. Productive fear pushes us to get out of our boxes and take meaningful risks that advance our growth. Nonproductive fear keeps us rooted in anxiety, worry, and stress.

12. *Is every day an opportunity to add to someone's happiness?* Even the smallest seeds of kindness can reap the greatest harvest. A smile, a light touch, or a helping hand can grow vast fields of love. Love is the driving force behind every gesture of

kindness. This love, which is the living presence of Spirit, empowers you to bestow kindness on yourself and others not for personal gain or accolades, but for the sheer thrill of alleviating someone else's pain for a moment or for a lifetime.
13. *What do you do when adversity strikes?* Are you even-minded and calm when things go wrong? Or do you have a meltdown and relinquish the calm center of peace within you?
14. *Are you grateful for whatever comes your way?* Do you recognize that everything is an invitation to deepen your connection with God and to grow, no matter how painful the situation may be?
15. *Do you feel all your feelings, including the pleasant ones and the painful ones?* Feeling your feelings means declining the use of excessive alcohol and recreational drugs, as well as avoiding any kind of addiction such as excessive shopping, gambling, sex, or working.

Be sure to keep this list handy and go over it several times. Consider how different your life would look if you incorporated these aspects into your daily living. How would the people in your life react if you were to have a bodhichitta attitude from this moment on? What would happen? How would you handle it? Are you willing to get attitude at any cost to honor your heart, soul, and all life on this planet? The bodhichitta path is one of courage, fearlessness, and love. Can you accept the invitation to walk the path of kindness for yourself and for our wounded world?

Appendix Two

Your Kindness Tool Kit

In the Joy workshops that I teach, I invite participants to go home and create a Joy Tool Kit. This is a kit that helps raise one's joy levels when they are low or depleted. We can apply this same concept to kindness and create a Kindness Tool Kit. Why create a Kindness Tool Kit? It is a method of raising your vibration and connecting to the well of compassion within, which is especially helpful whenever you see unkindness in the world or you are being unkind to yourself. This kit is a gentle reminder that goodness is one's inherent nature, and kindness and compassion are quite visible in the world today.

So how do you create a Kindness Tool Kit? The first step is to find a box or any beautiful container of your choice (many arts and crafts stores have lovely boxes). Then fill your box or container with reminders of kindness shown to you, kindness you have shown to others, or kindness you see in the world. For me, I have a photo of my bunny Jake, whom my petsitter rescued off a busy street and brought to my family. When Jake arrived, his neck was filled with botfly (a deadly parasite of rodents and rabbits), which nearly killed him. Fortunately, the vet removed the botfly and larvae, but a gaping hole remained in Jake's neck that had to be irrigated twice a day. Once we lovingly healed him, Jake lived a long, happy, healthy life and was a precious addition to our family.

Other examples of items for your Kindness Tool Kit might include inspirational passages, photographs, CDs, devotional books, meditation chanting players, stories of kindness from real life or whatever inspires you to cultivate spiritual practice for love and compassion.

In your kit, you might want to include a beautiful journal to record gestures of kindness you observe being offered to yourself or to others. Maybe get a special pen to write with in this sacred journal. What will you write? Insights, thoughts, and feelings that arise from your spiritual practice or from everyday living. The journal is also a place to jot down what you are grateful for (even what you are grateful for in the face of adversity). You can also record answers from these appendices or any thoughts and emotions that arise while reading this book and pondering the topics we covered.

Make your Kindness Tool Kit special and unique to you: kindness can start with kindness to yourself.

Appendix Three

What Authentic Kindness Feels Like

What does it feel like to live your life from a place of authentic kindness deep within your heart? Here's what you can expect when you walk the path of love and kindness.

- You live without judgment of other people or the decisions they make.
- You are free from the stronghold of the ego.
- You forgive easily and don't ruminate over the wrongdoings of others.
- You recognize how the law of karma works and sow seeds of love for a brighter tomorrow.
- You understand the impermanence of form and are released from the suffering that attachment brings.
- You give love freely and fully without asking for or expecting anything in return.
- You revere the interconnectedness of all of life (including people, animals, sea life, and nature) and know that these are extensions of your own self. Harming any part of nature becomes incomprehensible to you.

- You freely and generously give to others, whether in a tangible or intangible form, taking pleasure in giving without wanting anything in return.
- You live in the present moment at peace with whatever that looks like.
- You are in service to others in some way and do so with graciousness and delight.
- You let go of negative thoughts and replace them with life-affirming positive thoughts. This is because you know that your beliefs shape your experience.
- You realize that you are more than your physical body and stop berating or criticizing your physical appearance. No longer do you need validation from others about your looks, intelligence, or attributes.
- Your heart swells with love for sentient beings and you treat yourself and others with tenderness and care.
- You see the presence of God everywhere you look.
- You give yourself over to God each day as an instrument of expression.
- You don't try to fix other people; rather, you offer compassion and empathy to those who are suffering.
- You remain even-minded in the face of adversity.
- You abandon materialistic cravings naturally and effortlessly, knowing that connection to God brings everlasting peace and joy.
- You empty yourself of anything unlike God and feel the bubbles of infinite bliss that have always been inside of you.

Appendix Four

An Exploration of Oneness

In Chapter Two, we explored the meaning of oneness. Now let's apply these principles directly to your life. First, take a pen and paper in hand and answer these questions. Just let the answers come straight from your heart without editing or writing what you think the response should be. Next, review your answers and take them into your heart.

1. Think about the premise that God is oneness manifesting through all of creation—in all and through all making us aspects of the one life, one heart, one mind. What do you think about this statement? Do you agree that we are all one and that all of creation is interconnected? Can you see God's hand in all of nature? Explain your answer.
2. What would the world look like if we revered all of life including the plant and animal kingdom? What can you do to help support the reverence of all of life?
3. Explain your take on Jesus' statement, "I am the vine; you are the branches. Abide in me as I in you."
4. Go back and read the story about Snowflake in Chapter 2. What feelings arise in you after reading this? Is there any difference in the life force of a bunny, chicken, pig, insect, or human? Why or why not?

5. Every year, 60 billion land animals and 1,000 billion marine animals are slaughtered for humans to consume. Can you support the suffering and pain that these animals experience, knowing that animal flesh is not necessary for a healthful diet?
6. Make an action plan of how you can contribute to honoring all life on this planet. For example, growing a garden, eating a plant-based diet, adopting a rescue animal, volunteering at a nonprofit organization. Once you make your action plan, will you take your first steps toward putting this plan into practice?

Appendix Five

The Art of Forgiving

Think back to a time when you were betrayed, hurt, mistreated, or suffering in some way. Reflect on whether your wounds have healed or if they are still open and causing you pain.

1. Think about Patti's story at the end of Chapter 6 and how you felt reading this. Would you have forgiven the rapists if this had happened in your own life? Was Patti wise and kind or was she a doormat for forgiving? What would you have done if you were in her situation?
2. Bring to mind someone who you have trouble forgiving. What is the obstacle that is preventing you from doing so? What would your life look like if you could forgive and move on?
3. Is there something that you need to forgive yourself for? Journal about this and practice the lovingkindness meditation to expedite forgiveness in yourself and others.
4. What do you have to release or embrace in order to forgive?
5. List the benefits of forgiving.
6. List the effects of holding a grudge or plotting revenge on yourself and the other person.
7. How does the law of karma work when it comes to forgiveness?

Appendix Six

New Thinking Patterns

This book has presented viewpoints from various faith traditions, some that may resonate with you and others that may not. Perhaps you have embraced a new viewpoint or expanded your consciousness in some way. Take a look at the following chart to see how your thinking patterns have changed as a result of reading this book.

Old Way of Thinking:	New Thoughts:
I am the author of all that I do.	God uses me as an instrument of expression and is the author of all that I do.
My self is who I am and I exist as a solitary unit.	I am connected with all of life, and that same spark of divinity within me is within the entire sphere of creation.
When I suffer emotionally, I turn to pills, alcohol, spending, or whatever it takes to numb the pain.	I feel my feelings, all of them, and gently move through pain and suffering without artificial aid, knowing that greater growth and compassion comes from the experience.

Old Way of Thinking:	New Thoughts:
If a friend is suffering, I tell them, "It's all good," "It's your karma," or "It's God's will."	With compassion, I listen to others who are suffering and stay present with them through the pain without resorting to trite spiritual platitudes.
I believe that my physical body is who I am.	My physical body is the form through which Spirit expresses. I am much more than a physical body.
My world revolves around myself, my family, my friends, and coworkers.	Giving in service to others is one reason why I am here. My love expands out further than my inner circle of friends and relations.
I remember every wrong that has been done to me. I hold a grudge and am vengeful to those who have hurt me.	Realizing that holding a grudge only hurts me, not the offender, I forgive, release, and respond with love.
Fear of loss runs my life; after all, we live in a brutal world.	I am not attached to form and trust that I am eternally connected to a power of good.
I anger easily and am critical of others.	I use anger for a catalyst for effective change and stay even-minded in the face of turmoil.
My ego runs the show.	I have shifted from self-cherishing to focusing on giving lovingkindness to others.

Old Way of Thinking:	New Thoughts:
I hold onto tangible items because you never know when you will run out.	Lovingly I give to others knowing I live in an abundant universe.
I'm too busy to take time for myself because of the demands of my hectic life.	Spiritual practice comes easily for me. I carve out time for meditation, prayer, and self-reflection.

Appendix Seven

Taking the Vow

The bodhisattva vow is traditionally taken by Mahayana Buddhists to attain complete enlightenment for the sake of all sentient beings. You don't have to be a monk or a nun to make a vow to live a life in which kindness is your driving force. While there is a formal, sacred ceremony for Buddhists taking the vow, you can make this vow in your own heart.

To see if you are ready to embark on this path of authentic kindness, ask yourself:

1. *Am I willing to give up pettiness and judgment and expand my heart in a greater way?* A kind heart places no judgement on others or on oneself. Petty grievances take up heart space where kindness should dwell.
2. *Can I engage in regular spiritual practice to connect with the Divine Presence within?* People often ask doctors which exercise is the best one for health and well-being. The answer? The one that you will do. The same is true for spiritual practice. Select one that resonates with you and that you will actually do on a day-to-day basis.
3. *Is my consciousness unitive?* Do I see and feel the oneness of all creation? Do I love my neighbor as myself, realizing there

is no separation between any of us? Can I honor the lives of the animals and at least consider eliminating murdered beings from my diet?

4. *Have I relinquished attachment to form?* Do I understand that attachment to form causes all suffering? Can I accept that form is always changing and the one permanence in my life is God the good, the omnipotent?

5. *Will I follow my heart, releasing what anyone else will think or say about me?* It is not always easy to follow your heart because often, you have to take risks and leave the familiarity of life as you know it. The reward is great love, joy, and bliss when walking your authentic path.

Once you answer these questions and feel ready to take the bodhisattva vow, you may do so. The following vow is an example from the book *The Bodhisattva Path of Wisdom and Compassion* by Chogyam Trungpa. Read it aloud and allow the feelings of love and compassion to permeate your soul.

"I (state your name) am going to take the vow of a bodhisattva. From today onward until the attainment of enlightenment, I'm going to commit myself to the path of the bodhisattva lineage and practice the bodhisattva path. I am willing to be a bridge, boat, earth, water or fire. I am willing to be a slave, physician, path, highway, taxi, bus, airplane, whatever is needed. I am willing to commit myself to having people walk on me, sit on me, and use me. I am willing for people to be inside me or outside me. I am willing to

be like a big whale that could swallow somebody, swim across the water and spit them out. Anybody can use any part of my physical existence or psychological territory."

After taking the vow, you will notice yourself becoming more kind, gentle, compassionate, and loving. Yes, you will still experience emotions such as anger, but they won't overwhelm you and make you erupt like a volcano. Stepping out of ego consciousness preserves you as a calm center in the midst of a storm. The goal is to keep walking the spiritual path and attain enlightenment, not for the benefit of yourself but for the benefit of all. May you be blessed.

Endnotes

Chapter 1: The Search for Authentic Kindness

1. The Infinite Bliss Mode of Action is described on page 31 of *Live Your Joy: How to Awaken from Spiritual Slumber*, Monarch Press, 2007, by Barbara Gulbranson. Acting from this state is complete immersion in God. All activity is done from complete union with the Divine. Many have visions, and the direct experience of God as God can now be seen in everyone. In this state of awareness, we stay centered no matter what is going on around us, trusting in a power of good to pave the way as we surrender to serving the Divine. No storm or challenge can shake us as we are consciously living, moving, and breathing as an extension of God. No longer influenced by mass consciousness, we are intuitively united with the source of all good as we experience the ecstasy of living our oneness with God.

Chapter 2: The Magic of Oneness

1. The Drama Dance mode of action is described in *Live Your Joy: How to Awaken from Spiritual Slumber* by Barbara Gulbranson, Monarch Press, 2007, page 28.

Chapter 3: The Healing Power of Kindness

1. Positive Prayer is a five-step system of prayer developed by Dr. Ernest Holmes, the founder of Religious Science. He based this system of prayer on the way Jesus prayed. Positive Prayer is based on the principle that there is an indwelling Creative Intelligence that is all good and that our beliefs outpicture as conditions in our lives. Once we make a series of statements of truth, the law works to bring our desires to fruition. For the steps in Positive Prayer, see *Live Your Joy: How to Awaken from Spiritual Slumber,* by Barbara Gulbranson, Monarch Press, 2007, pp. 143–149.

Chapter 7: The Terrible Twos

1. The Infinite Bliss Mode of Action is described on page 31 of *Live Your Joy: How to Awaken from Spiritual Slumber,* Monarch Press, 2007, by Barbara Gulbranson.

Chapter 8: Cultivate Kindness

1. Paramahansa Yogananda, *The Yoga of Jesus,* Self-Realization Fellowship, 2007 p. 90.

Chapter 9: Empty Yourself

1. Jean-Yves Leloup, *The Gospel of Thomas: The Gnostic Wisdom of Jesus,* Inner Traditions, 1986, p. 120.

Resources

For information on:

U R Awesome Inc.
– www.urawesome.org

AHOWAN Traveling Spiritual Ministry
– www.ahowan.org

Live Your Joy Institute and publications
– www.liveyourjoy.org

Claudia Mulcahy books, publications and teachings
– www.CancerWhatToDoOrSay.com

Transcendental Meditation
– www.TM.org

Pure Land Buddhism
– www.amtbweb.org/purelandbuddhism.html

Kriya Yoga
– www.ananda.org/kriya-yoga

Centering Prayer
– www.centeringprayer.com

Acknowledgments

With deep gratitude I acknowledge the ones who supported me while making this book a reality. To my husband Jeff, for supporting me not just during the writing process but in all areas of my life. I thank him for understanding my divine urge to write and for providing me with everything I need to answer this sacred calling. To my daughter, Kim, the brilliant, beautiful, kindhearted woman who read drafts and gave precious insight into what's on these pages. She demonstrates the creative power within time and again and, by example, inspires me to fulfill my dreams. Thank you to Grace Hospice for the opportunity to work as a chaplain, for believing in me and enabling me to witness lovingkindness each day that I visited patients. I want to thank the monks of New Camaldoli Hermitage, Big Sur, California, who lovingly provided me with the heartfelt hymn that I so wanted to include in this book to inspire and uplift the readers. To all those willing souls who had the courage and kindness to share their deeply personal stories with me and the readers. I appreciate it. To Dr. Angelo Pizelo for being a constant source of support and giving me the opportunity to earn higher education degrees. To Mary McCarty, Bill Earle and their talented team. Most of all, thank you to the gurus, teachers, mystics and masters who I quoted in this book who have been my inspiration throughout the years. Thank you with all of my heart to God, the angels and archangels who are the real authors of this

Barbara Gulbranson

book. Their heavenly messages flowed through me onto the pages and I am deeply grateful to serve as an instrument in this way. With deep gratitude and love, thank you all.

About the Author

Barbara Gulbranson has been on a spiritual path throughout her entire lifetime. Her vision is to help alleviate suffering in individuals and ultimately in the world through lovingkindness. Her proven belief is that kindness is a powerful healing force to mend hearts, dry tears, and affect personal transformation in humankind and in all of the beings sharing the planet today.

Barbara is author of the critically acclaimed books *Live Your Joy: How to Awaken from Spiritual Slumber*, *How to Attract Your Soul Mate: the Secrets of Lasting Love*, and *Angel Talk: Five Easy Steps for Connecting with Your Angels*. She is also the founder and director of Live Your Joy Institute, a nonprofit church without walls. She is a speaker, spiritual counselor, workshop leader, and publisher of the *Joy Newsletter*.

Barbara believes that we are all interconnected and that by honoring, loving, and respecting all beings, our lives are lifted up and transformed. She believes that love and kindness to all is the key to ending the human condition of suffering and that we can achieve this type of transformation during our lifetimes. The key to healing and living in bliss consciousness is a simple spiritual practice as reflected in Barbara's writings and workshops. She uses her knowledge of spiritual principles and teachings from many faith traditions to assist the individual in transforming and awakening to live a life filled with peace, love, and joy.

Barbara Gulbranson

Barbara is an ordained minister and holds a Master's Degree in Religious Studies and a Doctorate of Divinity Degree from Emerson Theological Institute. She is available for speaking, workshops, coaching, and seminars.

CONTACT INFORMATION:

Visit www.liveyourjoy.org
or write to:

PO Box 1045
Granger, IN 46530

E-mail:
revbarbgulbran@cs.com

Also by Barbara Gulbranson:

Live Your Joy:
How to Awaken from
Spiritual Slumber

How to Attract Your Soul Mate:
The Secrets of Lasting Love

Angel Talk:
Five Easy Steps for Connecting
with Your Angels

Monarch Press

For more information about the author's publications, classes and speaking engagements, or to subscribe to the free *Joy Newsletter*, visit:

www.liveyourjoy.org

www.ingramcontent.com/pod-product-compliance
Lightning Source LLC
Chambersburg PA
CBHW070055080526
44586CB00013B/1068